CREATIVE
HOMEOWNER®

The Best of
Signature
Baths

CREATIVE HOMEOWNER®, Upper Saddle River, New Jersey

First published in book form in 2007 by

CREATIVE
HOMEOWNER®

A Division of Federal Marketing Corp.
Upper Saddle River, NJ

Text and photos © 2006 Magnolia Media Group

Signature Kitchens & Baths Magazine is published by Magnolia Media Group

VICE PRESIDENT & PUBLISHER: Timothy O. Bakke
PRODUCTION DIRECTOR: Kimberly H. Vivas
ART DIRECTOR: David Geer
BOOK LAYOUT & COVER DESIGN: Maureen Mulligan
EDITORIAL ASSISTANT: Nora Grace
INTERN: Kealan Bakke

Current Printing (last digit)
10 9 8 7 6 5

Manufactured in the United States of America

The Best of Signature Baths, First Edition
Library of Congress Control Number: 2007923436
ISBN-10: 1-58011-362-1
ISBN-13: 978-1-58011-362-5

CREATIVE HOMEOWNER®
A Division of Federal Marketing Corp.
24 Park Way
Upper Saddle River, NJ 07458
www.creativehomeowner.com

Contents

Some Basics

The Baths

Appendix

A FRESH OUTLOOK

PRACTICAL IDEAS FOR UPDATING WORN-OUT BATHS,

BY **CHRIS DREITH, CKD, CBD**

Small changes to your bath can brighten the space or transform the room. Baths by Walker Zanger (above) and VitrA (top right).

IMAGINE YOU'RE ON YOUR WAY HOME from work, stuck in traffic, dead tired. Your mind runs, and you find yourself fantasizing about your own personal retreat, a quiet bath, or an invigorating shower. When you finally reach home, you drag yourself through the house to your bathroom and swing open the door, and your bathroom looks as tired as you are. What can you do?

Renovating a bathroom can often be more complex than any other room renovation, but sometimes the simplest changes are all that is needed. First things first: Declutter. How many bottles of shampoo do you really need? Purge. Then decide what is needed to turn your bathroom into a tranquil retreat.

Small changes such as hanging fresh-colored towels, a shower curtain, a picture, or decorative mirror can painlessly brighten a room. Towel bars, toilet paper holders, or grab bars can be replaced with slightly more skill. (Make sure there is substantial backing in the walls.) Do some purposeful shopping and add a piece of furniture, such as a small cabinet, stool, or table. If you are crafty, you might find treasures to refurbish in consignment shops or antique stores. Rollout trash cans, pullout shelves, or drawer dividers for makeup or jewelry make life easier. Home centers, specialty bath shops, or Web sites such as *www.rev-a-shelf.com* stock a variety of convenience products.

If you're feeling a little more adventurous, paint the walls and ceiling. Just be careful to prep the surfaces. Your local specialty paint store can help you select the necessary products. Consider using either PermaWhite paint from Zinnzer, which has a mildew-resistant additive, or purchase Mild-Ex to add to your own paint. Just keep in mind: sometimes the additive has an unpleasant odor, which is completely normal. Add a teaspoon of vanilla extract to the gallon to make it less pungent, and then let your creative juices flow. Have your kids dip their hands in bright-colored paints and decorate the walls with their handprints. Many specialty paint stores offer classes that teach a variety of finishing techniques. When you tire of the color, simply replace it with a different hue. Wallpapering takes a little more patience and skill. Once again, prepping is important. Be sure to select paper that is made for bathrooms, otherwise seams will open and the paper will peel.

For another effortless update, consider replacing the knobs on your cabinetry. Notting Hill Decorative Hardware (*www.nottinghill-usa.com*) offers elegant options; Dekkor (*www.dekkorinc.com*) crafts contemporary pieces from metal and glass. Even toilet levers can be changed. Look for those in plumbing supply showrooms.

Vanity countertops can be found in standard sizes—many with sinks included—at home centers and kitchen and bath showrooms. To view a variety of countertop materials, visit *www.lippertcorp.com* or *www.swanstone.com*. If you choose to replace your countertop and sink, you'll need to replace the faucet as well. If you are purchasing a prefabricated counter, make sure the holes drilled for the faucet will match your faucetry of choice. You may also want to see about adding a filtered water system for healthy drinking water.

With a little more expertise, consider replacing plumbing fixtures. Changing a standard showerhead to a handheld is easy. Substituting a toilet will take more time and muscle, but an updated commode may be exactly what your bathroom needs. For those adventurous do-it-yourselfers, several home centers offer classes for basic plumbing or electrical change-outs. The less venturesome will want to skip the class and hire a professional.

A professional designer can suggest design options you may not want to tackle yourself. Perhaps you'd like your home to be ADA-compliant without looking institutional. Maybe your dream bathroom includes an audio/visual/security system. Perhaps you share your personal retreat with others. How do you ensure all your wants and needs are met? Find a Certified Bath Designer (CBD) to assist you in the remodeling process. CBDs make it a point to stay abreast of hot products and contemporary designs. A list of CBDs is available from the National Kitchen and Bath Association at 908-852-0033 or online at *www.NKBA.com*. «

POINT, CLICK, INSPIRE

ONLINE LINKS FOR HOT PRODUCTS

Innovative bath products are transforming what was once a utilitarian room into an indulgent escape from the demands of everyday activities. Here's a peek at what's new in the bath industry, along with suggestions for where to find these fun products online.

» TV mirrors are bringing ultra-modern entertainment to the bathroom. Turn the system on for a convenient viewing location; turn it off for a complete mirror reflection. Lie back and switch channels with your floating remote control. For the original TV mirror, see *www.seuratvmirror.com*.

» Stay warm with heated towel warmers and in-floor heating. Towel warmers can dry off your swimsuit and warm up your mittens. Visit Zehnder's radiators at *www.zehnderamerica.com* or check out Engineered Glass Products' heated glass towel warmers at *www.egpglass.com*. Similarly, flooring systems placed under floor tiles take the edge off cold mornings. See *www.warmlyyours.com*.

» Lights no longer merely brighten a space. Tubs such as those manufactured by Jason Hydrotherapy (*www.jasoninternational.com*) feature therapeutic underwater lights to create a healing chromatherapy experience. KWC offers faucets with LED lighting that changes from blue to red as the water heats (*www.KWC.com*).

» Toto USA boasts a toilet/bidet combo with a heated seat and built-in exhaust fan. Visit *www.totousa.com*.

» For the ultimate shower, Jacuzzi has designed shower towers with body sprays and handheld showerheads that also dispense a gentle stream of heated air to dry bathers (*www.jacuzzi.com*). Steam units can transform an ordinary bath into an extraordinary experience (*www.ThermaSol.com*).

To see the real thing, contact your nearest Certified Bath Designer or check out the designers listed in this book.

If you're looking for
something more exotic in
the way of materials, you
may want to cast an eye
toward PSC.

BATHTUB BLISS

Since the beginning of time, a hot bath has offered up one of life's simplest pleasures. More than a way to get clean, a long bath in a good tub is a time-tested ticket to relaxation and rejuvenation. Fortunately, today's bathtub manufacturers are pairing this down-to-earth delight with innovation, efficiency, and aesthetics.

"The bath has become the great American escape of today," says Lenora Campos, Ph.D., public relations manager for TOTO, the world's largest plumbing manufacturer with more than $3.4 billion in annual sales and 80 affiliated production facilities around the globe. "Americans are adopting the European attitude toward the bath as a spa. The days of the bath as a merely utilitarian room are gone."

INNOVATIVE TUBS

According to Campos, the bathroom is now a place for solitude and relaxation. Therefore, it demands the height of luxury, such as that delivered by TOTO's new Nexus suite. Bathers soaking in the Nexus Air Tub can revitalize themselves by incorporating two primal elements into their soak: air and light. The Nexus Champagne Bubble System contains special, strategically placed jets that target the body's pressure points, while tiny effervescent bubbles cling to and caress the skin. The Nexus bathing experience also includes remote-controlled chromatherapy, which uses a sequence of colored light to stimulate different psychological and physiological responses.

Jacuzzi, the granddaddy of whirlpool bathing, brings forth its own angle on chromatherapy as it introduces its Illumatherapy fiber optic lighting system—the first ever fiber optic lighting system built inside a bath's whirlpool jets. "Light and color affect how we feel, and Jacuzzi's system is a first for this industry, enabling consumers to personalize their whirlpool bath experience," says Ken Baker, president, Jacuzzi Whirlpool Bath. Jacuzzi's Illumatherapy fiber optic feature will first be available on its Bellavista tub.

Other noteworthy therapeutic innovations include MTI Whirlpool's hydrotherapy jets, purported to create "a perfect mix of air and water for deep tissue massage." A variety of MTI's thermo-air massage systems also offer a lighter, full-body massage. MTI's LED underwater lighting is available with constant color or preset programs for its own brand of soothing or invigorating lighting effects.

TIMELESS TUBS WITH MODERN TWISTS

The unmatched elegance of freestanding baths has caught the eye and imaginations of consumers and designers alike. Gone are the cast-iron, claw-footed tubs of our great-grandmothers. Today we're talking sleek and sophisticated, with state-of-the-art amenities. MTI Whirlpool's newest product, the Oasis, is a contemporary, freestanding tub offering an "exhilarating" air-bath massage. If you like bathing á deux—this improved throwback comes in two sizes for single or multiple bathers.

Speaking of multiple bathers, the MTI Eternity offers two bathers a roomy dual bathing experience complete with integral armrests and MTI's full range of custom options. But if

(Above) MTI Whirlpool's tubs contain thermo-air massage systems for the most relaxing bathing experience imaginable. (right) The recycled plastics in Durat avant-garde tubs give the finished surface depth.

it's seclusion you seek in your bathing experience, you may want to consider hydrotherapy for one with MTI's Solitude, providing a cradling shape lumbar support that leaves no quarter for bathroom interlopers.

Not only is the spa-like atmosphere becoming the hallmark of America's most-wanted bathrooms, manufacturers are also finding that the little things mean a lot to today's savvy consumers. Amenities garnering consumers' attention include the balanced air-and-heat distribution offered by Jacuzzi's new Pure-Air Bath Next Generation system, which incorporates new and revamped air bath technology with more than 100 air channels for an even 360-degree air distribution.

For a more avant-garde twist on standard tub styling, Durat Design by Tonester Ltd. of Finland offers a line of bathroom tubs with an emphasis on the emotional beauty of the material. Durat—a solid surface material containing approximately 50 percent recycled plastics—is available in 46 standard colors. The sophistication of Durat lies in its silky warm feeling and the interesting impression of depth in its finish. A Durat bathtub will add modern emotion to any bathroom.

CREATING EFFICIENT COMBINATIONS
Whether it's constraints of time, space, or bath vs. shower indecision, a combination bath and shower can solve a multitude of dilemmas without having to give up amenities. MTI's new ergonomically

designed Bella bath offers the comfort and relaxation of a soaker with the efficient convenience of a shower option. Bella comes in more than 30 colors of high-gloss, Lucite cast acrylic.

If it's tub space you're after, or a compromise between a bathtub and full-fledged hot tub, the MTI Rotunda may be just the gateway to relaxation you've been seeking. With its simple round design and additional two feet of soaking depth, the Rotunda offers luxurious options, including any combination of MTI's whirlpool-air, bath-soaker options.

The latest innovation most deserving of the term, "revolutionary combination" may be Jacuzzi's Summer Rain Shower Series with its Ambient Air Body Dry System. This concept, once relegated to drive-thru car washes, has climbed to a new incarnation, featuring 12 powerful, soothing air jets that shoot preheated air from a center shower column to air-dry bathers quickly without lifting a towel. The temperature and airflow of these fully adjustable jets are controlled via a central panel to suit personal and seasonal preferences.

CAPITALIZING ON AESTHETICS
Bringing nature's beauty into the home is a concept that has grown steadily in popularity, and the bathroom makes no exception. As architects and designers have created prettier spaces, manufacturers have responded with products like MTI's new Primm bath—an acrylic freestand-

ing soaker tub supported by a handcrafted cast iron frame that incorporates a graceful sculptured profusion of cattails.

For even more of a Zen connotation, take a look at the Bamboo Tub from Diamond Spas, Inc. This freestanding stainless-steel Japanese soaking tub is creatively encircled by a bamboo design that seeks to create a Zen-like atmosphere. This 42" x 42" x 35" tub creates a strong artistic statement in conjunction with the unbeatable durability of materials. A similar product providing a slightly different feel is the Japanese Copper Soaker Bath, also from Diamond Spas. Designed to create a tranquil, relaxing bathing environment, this stylish circular tub measures 42" x 42" x 35". Fashioned from raw copper, it also features a bench seat for comfort and function and a curved top ledge that adds artistic charisma to complete the unique bath statement.

For a relaxing rendezvous with Old World Mediterranean beauty, you may want to acquaint yourself with the Acryline® Mediterranean— a large oval island bathtub designed to be reminiscent of the ancient architecture of the Mediterranean region. With its raised head-and-neck supports and sloping backrests at both ends, the Mediterranean offers a balanced aesthetic beauty that can be appreciated from both outside and within the tub. The Mediterranean is available as a soaking bath or with Acryline's warm air hydromassage therapy systems. Because the Acryline

Mediterranean is visually inviting from rim to floor, it makes for a versatile choice for almost any island location within a large bathroom.

CARRYING AESTHETICS A STEP FURTHER

If you're looking for something more exotic in the way of materials, you may want to cast an eye toward PSC, America's sole importer for Image, Nevobad, Logo, and the MS Collection. PSC is the only distributor on the market to develop a collection of bathroom products made of wood, crystal, and luxury stones.

Image, a PSC Company based in France, presents sleek, wooded tubs that are true works of art. Each comes stamped with an identification number linked to a 5-year warranty. All Image tubs can be customized and are available in a dark African Iroko wood or a light American maple.

For stunning, contemporary bathtub designs that are as pretty to behold as they are to bathe in, check out Nevobad, a PSC company based in Germany that presents the "complete solution for the bathroom", combining crystal with metal, marble, and wood. Nevobad's Cocoon presents a clean, rectangular design of stone and crystal accented by black stair-stepped polished accents and metal fixtures.

Thanks to the innovative designs of these manufacturers, the days of a bath being merely a bath are behind us forever. So light some candles, put on some music and plan your daily retreat into a relaxing haven of your own creation. «

(left) Nexus offers lavish pampering in combining air and light therapy. (above) This Japanese Copper Soaker Bath by Diamond Spas creates a relaxing Zen-like atmosphere.

LET IT RAIN

Relaxing, therapeutic, and natural all describe the experience of showers and baths in contemporary culture. Is there anything better than stepping into a shower that indulges your design taste and creates a relaxing experience all within itself? As with any other room in the home, bathrooms are designed not only for functionality but also for beauty. Therefore, shower design must be functional, but it must also encompass natural design elements to complete the experience.

Using stone in conjunction with light, glass and water can transform an individual into a heightened state of relaxation and can allow the bather to enjoy the beauty of the shower as if it were a decorative fixture. No longer a room to be closed from prying eyes, bathrooms have instead become a design-worthy entity of the home meant to create release and enjoyment.

ELEMENTS OF THE EARTH

Stone, glass, and metals are all used to create a harmonious space that indulges the senses and body. Design is often influenced by nature to develop a space that connects the individual with the experience. Today's bath and shower manufacturers have recognized the organic aspects of design and have created products to deliver that experience.

Handmade by second and third generation mosaic artists in Israel, Minos Mosaics is the top-of-the-line collection in the extensive Ann Sack's offering. Each tile piece is a basis of organic elements, such as water, shells, flora, and the sun, and is applied as it appears in nature. Shell and water inspired pieces are applied on the floor, floral pieces closer to the lower half, and sun and sky pieces closer towards the ceiling.

Celesta Luxury Shower Enclosures encompass the natural materials of glass and light, and serve to create a feeling of openness. Celesta's products showcase beautiful tile work and provide the consumer with a luxury glass enclosure experience. The LX935 Model eliminates the large, bulky feeling once created by many glass enclosures and accentuates an open, natural feeling, allowing shower aesthetics to be appreciated and eliminating feelings of containment.

A THERAPEUTIC EXPERIENCE

Stepping into a beautifully designed shower is sensory therapy within itself, but design cannot compare to the appeal of cascading water from a well-designed showerhead.

MAAX, a world-leading manufacturer of bathroom and spa solutions, is embracing the minimalist approach to bathroom trends and is applying organic elements to enhance the shower experience. Their new shower massage systems, in the URBAN Series and the Rainmax Rainmaker, unite the sensual science of strategically positioned water flow with streamlined design to define beauty and efficiency.

Being one of the most relaxing parts of our day, the shower no longer must be an assemblage of various coordinated parts, but a genuine object in its own right. Such is the

Kohler (left) continues to develop new color dimensions for the bath. Kohler Vapour™ colors allow homeowners to create their own personality in the bath.

philosophy that inspired Isy by Zucchetti shower columns. Three sophisticated models each appear to be taken from the idea of showering in waterfalls.

This waterfall idea is further developed with the addition of a thermostatic mixer to control the jets; a flat, very large nozzle for a relaxing, soothing rain-like jet; or a small, cylindrical nozzle to produce an intense jet of water for daily well-being. All three versions make a practical, handsome shower that proves to be both versatile and a true pleasure.

The waterfall sensation can also be found in rain showerheads that deliver a relaxing shower spray designed to envelope the body in falling water. Grohe's Retro Rainshower adds a touch of nostalgia to shower designs and is the perfect touch to enhance the raw shower experience. The 8-inch diameter showerhead features 120 spray nozzles to leave no "dry" zones. Similar to rain drops, the nozzles rejuvenate the body with a traditional, clean approach.

Jaclo's Frescia handheld shower delivers a similar experience. The Frescia has three full functions, including a full rain spray, an invigorating massage, and the new nebulizing mist spray. The nebulizing mist spray stimulates the fine, cloudlike spray found in steam showers and vaporizing units.

INNOVATIONS IN THE SHOWER

Each of us loves a hot shower, but how many of us dislike the shock of cold air that snaps us back to reality? Fortunately, bathers can now go from shower to shirt without lifting a towel. Jacuzzi Whirlpool Bath has revolutionized the shower experience in its new product line, Summer Rain, which includes a special option, the Ambient Air Body Dry System, also described on page 10. This unique feature provides head-to-toe drying and is delivered through an Ambient Air Body Dry System with 12 powerful, soothing air jets designed in a center shower column. After showering, warm air enables bathers to dry off quickly, literally without lifting a towel. Temperature airflow can be controlled through a control panel. A pre-heat cycle ensures instant warm air after the shower.

The Summer Rain Series, a trend on today's bathroom preferences, is based on the idea that more and more people are replacing single showers with more spacious showers for two.

"Bathrooms are bigger, and people want to have the luxury of a spacious shower for themselves or the opportunity to shower with their mate," said Aly Johnson, vice president, Jacuzzi Baths and Showers.

Maax (left) Shower options; Celeste (right) Luxury Glass Enclosures.

Maax (left) shower enclosures and shower systems; Grohe (middle) Amera shower system; Ondine (right) Riva Shower.

As showers get more spacious, showerheads are becoming more luxurious. The Waterhill Collection, by Showhouse by Moen, is an innovative look at the luxury shower experience. The Waterhill spa offers the ultimate escape, transforming your daily shower into an experience unlike any other. The Five Function Exact Temp Vertical Spa set has a pressure-balanced, thermostatic control with five function diverters that can be placed anywhere on the shower wall. Installing two Waterhill Spa packages on either side of the shower will create the ultimate water-caressing experience. Imagine relaxing after a long day as water gently massages your back, legs, arms, and feet all at once. Ahh, heaven! An 8-inch showerhead with pressurized water delivery and sculptured arm allows for perfectly controlled pressure regardless of line pressure. The wall-mounted hand shower allows for more complete control.

Noteworthy also in innovation is Swanstone's Shell Shower, the shower without a curtain or door. First introduced 40 years ago, the Shell Shower is reintroduced to the Swanstone line in recognition of the company's four decades of innovative design. The product's unique curved shape eliminates the need for a curtain or door, not to mention

the absence of hard corners keeps dirt and grime from accumulating.

No longer designed out of necessity, designers are now creating showers with the luxurious shower experience in mind. With so many options including tile, natural stone, and the many innovations within the industry, showers are becoming the choice place for retreat and relaxation. When choosing a shower, be careful to give consideration to the entire entity rather than one or two simple fixtures. What would make your shower experience complete? Slate, glass walls, perhaps granite flooring? With such diverse products available, it's up to you to choose how to finish your design, whether through shower columns, multiple jet streams, or a single showerhead. «

The Riverbath (round and quadrangle) from Kohler envelops the senses with different natural elements–waterfall, rapids, or a gently flowing current. It's where nature meets nurture.

total joy
WHIRLPOOL BATHS

ONCE YOU'VE EXPERIENCED the incredible sensation of relaxing in a jetted tub (and the way your body feels afterward), it's only natural to want your own whirlpool bath. Going to the spa is fine, but there are all those details. How simple just to slip away for an hour and emerge refreshed and rejuvenated.

So what do you do first? As with most endeavors, check your budget. There's a wide price range, so you'll find something that's just right. And spend some time, as well, contemplating the space you have available. Then, because this is a major project, work with a professional designer to make sure your finished bath is exactly what you wanted.

Maybe you think a scarlet heart-shaped tub is a little over the top (but MTI has a gorgeous one available) and find a plain white rectangle just "too vanilla" (although Kohler's ultra-deep Sok will change your mind). There are so many choices in between these two that you'll have no trouble finding the shape and color of your dreams. Growing in popularity are corner-placed tubs, which enlarge your field of possibilities for placement and evoke a cozy, sheltered feeling at the same time.

The style of your bathroom blends with the style of your entire home, and jetted tubs are fashioned to match period, traditional, and contemporary looks. Tubs can be faced with myriad materials. Custom bath enclosures, such as those supplied by Duschqueen, Inc., can transform your tub and provide water-tight and/or steam-tight spaces. So you can lie back, pretend you're the emperor of everything, let the moving waters massage your body and

The Zen-like simplicity of a deep bath present in Kohler's Sok—water continuously overflows the tub's rim, pleasing the senses. Float in a cocoon of chin-high warmth—the tub is 75 inches long and 24½ inches deep.

spirit—and still be sure that every element is in total visual accord.

Jetted tubs for two provide the ultimate in relaxation, a perfect way for busy professional couples to end a day in peace and tranquility. These can also fit into a corner, so if a double tub is high on your wish list, space may not be a problem at all. If your idea of luxury is soaking in the whirlpool with your sweetie while watching television or movies on DVD or listening to tapes or CDs, there's a tub that combines all of those elements.

If you have children, you'll find bathtime a joy with a whirlpool bath. If they have their own bathroom, they can have their own tub. Child-size baths are a pleasure for kids and parents alike.

So many options, sizes, styles, colors, and shapes are available. So many features are hidden behind the scenes to assure you years of trouble-free service. A whirlpool bath should relax, pamper, and de-stress your life—not be a constant cause of repairs. Today's technology gives you that ease of operation, leaving you free to choose based on just what you like, just what fits into your grand scheme. Let's go shopping for whirlpools, and look forward to all the hours of pure luxury and repose.

THE LITTLE EXTRAS

You've chosen your new whirlpool bath, it's installed, and you've enjoyed the relaxation and therapeutic benefits that it provides. With the major element in place, you can take a few more steps, add the little extras that will turn your bathroom into a sanctuary.

Set the stage with lighting. In addition to task lighting, install mood lighting in unexpected areas, perhaps above a soffit, along with a wall light by the tub so you can read while you soak. Put all lights on dimmers so you can adjust brightness.

Choose a relaxing color. This is an individual choice. You might prefer deeper shades to give your bathroom a cloistered, den-like appeal, or gentle pastels to create an open, airy feeling. In a master bath, feng shui practitioners might suggest incorporating shades of pink—the color of partnership. This doesn't have to be a sugary pink, by the way. It can be bright raspberry, a grayed pink, or one of this season's hottest colors—an almost-coral, dusky salmon.

Invest in cushy linens. Towels are among your bathroom's more affordable necessities, as well as a way to add color and texture to the space. Choose generously sized towels

Part of the Gallery™ Collection from Jacuzzi, the Gallery Corner whirlpool is an ideal fit for most bathrooms and is easy to maintain and clean.

in thick terry cloth or luxurious Egyptian cotton. Include a soft bath mat and an oversized, plush terry robe.

Wire your room for sound. A small portable stereo system, housed safely away from water, will let you enjoy your favorite music while you relax. If you love the sound of running water, include a small fountain in the decor.

Introduce soothing scents. Like the feng shui advice, you may take the benefits of aromatherapy as seriously or as lightly as you like, but we all like pleasing fragrances. Some calm, some energize, and others bring back memories.

Warm things up. To keep yourself cozy while you dry off, consider an overhead light with a heating element. Another simple luxury: a heated towel bar.

Give yourself an overhead view. Something as simple as a ceiling painted in a restful color or as elaborate as a trompe l'oeil design of a cloudy sky will add to the room's appeal.

Make it personal. A tubside table with a book, seashells you found on the beach, and some plants add a special touch to your private spa. You'll find that plants flourish in the humid atmosphere. «

PERSONAL SPA
Like so many other things, the bathroom as we once knew it has evolved. From a room of necessity, it has morphed into a sanctuary—a retreat where one can go to leave the fast-paced world.

(Top) Jacuzzi's Fuzion Series bathtubs feature a bold design with a modern twist. The natural wood deck contributes to the tranquil feeling of a personal home spa. (Left) The two-person model features a dual system that allows each user to perfectly customize their experience. An overflow feature allows for the tub to be fully filled.

BATHTUB BLISS

The perfect place to start is with your bathtub. Driftwood Handmade Baths manufactures individually crafted, handmade wooden bathtubs. The company's designer, Finbarr Duggan, draws upon his training as a bridge designer to create sturdy, functional, and attractive designs. Choose from a palette of woods for a tub that will perfectly meld with your bathroom decor. Driftwood's tubs bring a touch of nature's tranquility to your bathroom.

"Bathrooms should be a shrine to relaxation," Duggan said. The tubs have a strong design, while remaining beautifully simplistic, never overpowering the feel of the room. Besides looking great, Driftwood's wooden baths are built with the same technology used to build boats, so they will never weep or leak. They are insulated to maintain heat during bathing and are even a boon for the environment with their carbon lock-in feature.

OLD FAVORITE, NEW TWISTS

Another leader in the spa-like bathroom trend is Jacuzzi, which has taken the driver's seat in this arena with its Luxury Collection. "Jacuzzi's Luxury Collection baths will immerse the consumer in a total spa experience," said Phil Weeks, president of Jacuzzi Bath Division. The company's new tubs feature an experience dubbed "Salon," an innovative combination of an old favorite, Jacuzzi's original whirlpool bath, along with its new technology, Pure Air. The Pure Air feature circulates air through a 900-watt heated air blower and releases it through a parallel track of small air holes located at the bottom of the bath. Jacuzzi's patented 360° Balanced Air Flow ensures that the heat and the air are consistently moving, thus eliminating cold spots. The Pure Air bath is designed to be a more relaxing, soothing experience in contrast to the invigorating effect of the whirlpool. Based on your needs, you can select the whirlpool

function or the Pure Air Bath. The features can even be used simultaneously.

A notable member of the Luxury Collection family is the Fuzion Series. These fashionable tubs boast clean architectural lines with a modern edge. Along with the Salon experience, the Fuzion series features such lavish perks as the Dual Zone capability, available in the two-person model, which allows each user to adjust the power of the whirlpool flow. The patented SilentAir induction system creates a quieter experience. The tub boasts an exotic wood deck, available in light teak or dark wenge.

LET IT RAIN

The modern shower can also be just as much of a retreat as the bath. Kohler's new Vivacia Rain showerhead has a large face that immerses the user in a relaxing, gentle rain. The showerhead can be installed on the ceiling or on the wall by using a 90-degree shower arm. Another great innovation from Kohler is the WaterTile. The sleek water tiles are designed to be nearly flush with the wall, ridding the shower space of visual clutter. The WaterTiles can be arranged in almost any configuration: on the wall, on the ceiling or even at the intersection of the two. The tiles are actually adjustable, allowing you to alter the direction of the spray. As a companion to the WaterTiles, Kohler offers the wall-mount showerhead, which is wrapped in a sleeve and embodies the same technology and sleek design as the WaterTile. Both the WaterTile body sprays and showerhead are offered in two spray intensities. Choose from a 54-nozzle spray for a soothing shower or a 22-nozzle spray for a more stimulating experience.

STEAM CLEAN

In addition to exciting showerheads and other options, homeowners can now experience a great luxury within the comforts of their own dwelling: steam. "Saunas provide feelings of relaxation, rejuvenation and may reduce the effects of a busy lifestyle," said Charles Monteverdi, president of Mr. Steam. The

Sedona shower from Jacuzzi includes steam benefits, as well as shower features. Along with a glass door enclosure and an integrated seat, the Sedona has another special benefit: touch pad control panel with a built-in timer. What does this mean for you? Waking every morning to a preheated shower.

As the demand for luxurious baths increases, so does the product offering. "Throughout the years we have seen our product offerings transform from extras to essentials," Monteverdi said. Mr. Steam systems come standard with a uniquely designed steam head for quieter, softer steam. Also available is the AutoFlush drain, which drains water after each use and introduces fresh water prior to the next steambathing experience. Mr. Steam also provides a way to customize the experience with In-Shower TEMPO controls. Available features include programmable time, temperature settings, and a digital display.

ICING ON THE CAKE

Despite the availability of these lavish options, it's important to keep in mind that it's the small touches that truly say indulgence. Take for example Jacuzzi's Radiant Floor Heating Mat. Unobtrusive and discreetly hidden beneath the floor's surface, the Heating Mat eliminates the need for unsightly heating units or radiators. Additionally, the Private Lounge Bath Cart from Villeroy & Boch is an attractive, convenient mobile cube where you can place all of your bath essentials, allowing you to always have them within reach. And for a delightfully toasty post-bathing experience, Wesaunard's new towel warmers keep your towels warm and are available in a variety of designs, such as Victorian, Futurama, and the swirled Boz.

With so many options available, all that remains is to choose what best fits you and your lifestyle. According to Duggan, "Style is all about expression of individuality." «

(Left) Kohler's custom showering enables each user to customize their showering experience. The company's WaterTiles fit nearly flush with the wall, and the user can adjust the direction of the spray to receive the exact water coverage desired.

Universal Design

THE CLIENTS FOR THIS BATH PROJECT came into the showroom with the universal question, "How can I have a functional bath in such a small space?" In addition, they also desired a bath that would serve seniors and/or the handicapped.

The original space measured 5 x 9½ feet with a typical tub, water closet, small vanity, and small linen closet. A long, narrow closet measuring 3 x 9½ feet was situated next to the bath. To expand the room's size, the partition between these two rooms was removed to create a new space of 8½ x 9½ feet.

A major decision was made to eliminate the tub and implement a shower only. A 30-inch wide shower door was designed to open in or out. Double drains were built to accelerate the draining of excess water and to prevent slipping. A built-in shower seat was eliminated to provide space for a portable seat, which enables a second person to bathe a handicapped person.

A large vanity was included with two bowls and specialized storage for the homeowners. The granite countertop consists of two levels for wall storage to prevent water from splashing onto the wood cabinetry. A cabinet over the water closet creates extra storage. Task and general lighting, accessories and mirrors, custom wall and ceiling finishes, and artwork were added to complete this unique design. «

DESIGNER

Terry Cunningham
Kitchen Gallery
1034 Woodland Avenue
Knoxville, TN 37917
865-524-3457

SPECIAL FEATURES

Old English design; raised countertops; deep sinks; large shower door opens in or out; two drains in shower to prevent standing water and slipping

DIMENSIONS

9' x 9'

PRODUCTS USED

Tile: Winco
Cabinetry: Kitchen Gallery cabinetry
Mirrors: Custom
Sink(s): Corian
Toilet: Kohler
Shower Door: Custom glass
Showerhead: Grohe
Sink Faucets: Grohe
Shower Faucets: Grohe
Vanity Tops: Granite
Lights: Recessed
Drawer Pulls: Top Knobs

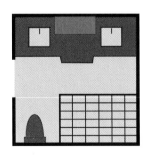

PHOTOGRAPHER: STEVE WHITSITT

Grand Solutions

DESIGNER
Sandra Rodriguez, CKD
L & S Interiors
1130 N. Kramaer Blvd,
Suite D.
Anaheim, CA 92806
714-998-8477

SPECIAL FEATURES
Limestone tile floor with
mosaic border; limestone
tile shower with bronze
sculpture rose deco tile;
cherry cabinets and
framed mirror; angled
Corner Tub

DIMENSIONS
13'3" x 11'9"

PRODUCTS USED
Tile: Honed Limestone,
Anatolia 12 x 12 inches
Cabinetry: Merit Cherry,
Rhode Island Stain with
Chocolate Chalk
Mirrors: L & S Interiors
Sink(s): Kohler, Caxton
Tub: MTI Whirlpool Tub,
Interlude II
Toilet: Toto
Showerhead:
Delta Victorian
Collection in Bronze
Sink faucets:
Delta Victorian
Collection in Bronze
Shower faucets:
Delta Victorian
Collection in Bronze
Vanity tops: Honed
Limestone, Anatolia
Drawer pulls: Top Knobs,
Limestone

THE TIME ARRIVED for the owners of this Irvine, California, home to update their simple, cramped bathroom into a room with a more elegant flare. To accomplish this, they contacted Sandra Rodriguez, CKD, of L & S Interiors in Anaheim, California.

The homeowners wanted a bathroom that felt more spacious without increasing the size of the master suite, and Rodriguez found several ways to gain space.

She enlarged the shower by removing a mechanical lift from behind it. The larger shower, coupled with the use of clear glass, gave a grand appearance to this seemingly larger room. The homeowners also wanted a larger whirlpool tub, which was placed in a corner to give the room a dramatic angle. The double vanity cabinets were designed in cherry with a rich, dark brown stain. Accents such as solid-cherry framed mirrors and crown molding give the vanity the look of furniture.

The direction of the commode and the door swing of the toilet were altered to add floor space. Limestone was selected for the floors, shower, and countertop to give the bathroom a classic look. The floor is 12 x 12-inch limestone tile with a tumbled-marble mosaic border. The shower uses the same 12 x 12 limestone, with the addition of 6 x 6 moonstone set on the diagonal with sculptured rose-metal tile embellishments.

"I feel like I'm staying in a fancy hotel every time I enter the bathroom," the homeowner said. «

A City View

Though this bathroom features stunning views, the homeowner was challenged with devising a design that might take advantage of the panorama without hindering the reflection in the mirror when getting ready. To help solve this dilemma, he opted to suspend mirrors from the ceiling. This solution opened up a beautiful wall of windows with views to the city outside.

The carefully planned bathroom also features gorgeous elements within. An infinity tub by Kohler occupies the center of the room; the tub is housed in a limestone slab and rests in front of the glass-enclosed shower. Two toilet closets, separated by a cabinet and frosted glass, provide the residents with needed privacy. Ample storage abounds within the room; walnut cabinetry comprises the storage compartments and contributes to the overall appeal of the space.

The sink vanity stretches against the wall with the view, and two sleek sink vessels sit atop a 4-inch stone slab. Beneath, grouted river rock butts up against the square limestone flooring. The same river rock also adorns the shower walls. And for the utmost in luxury, peek inside the cabinet to find a mini fridge located directly beneath a Samsung HDTV plasma monitor. «

DESIGNER
Nicole Sassaman Designs

DIMENSIONS
20' x 30'

PRODUCTS USED
Cabinetry: Walnut
Counter/floors: Stone tiles, rocks
Mirrors: Custom
Sink(s): Duravit
Faucet(s): Philippe Starck
Tub: Kohler
Shower/bath fixtures: Grohe
Toilet: Toto

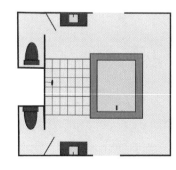

Tranquil Retreat

WHEN NICOLE SASSAMAN RENOVATED her Beverlycrest estate, she opted to design a show-stopping bathroom utilizing innovative products. Because the residence serves as the designer's own home, she wanted to create an architecturally appealing space with a Zen-like atmosphere—a room to which she could retreat to find some solace from her hectic pace.

Sassaman began the project in October 2003 and finished in June 2004. The lengthy remodel was due to the fact that she added a total of 3,000 additional square feet to the home. During the process, the bathroom presented its own set of design dilemmas. Most notably, she was challenged with finding unique materials for the bathroom that would work with the rest of the house while elevating the bathroom to showpiece status.

Sassaman solved the problem by choosing to complete the shower with a Walker Zanger tile that is typically used for outdoor applications. By thinking outside the box and bringing the tile inside, she successfully created a stunning bathroom that features the creative use of materials. If you want to apply similar design principles to your own space, Sassaman advises homeowners to think creatively before rushing out to pick tile or stone. The shower is one of the most expensive and messiest projects in the bathroom, so choose wisely! «

DESIGNER
Nicole Sassaman Designs

DIMENSIONS
7' x 12'

PRODUCTS USED
Tile: Walker Zanger
Cabinetry: Custom mahogany w/ glass laminate
Mirrors: Justo Gonzales Glass Works
Sink(s): Kohler
Faucet(s): Newport Brass
Toilet: Kohler
Shower: Walker Zanger stone
Shower door: Glass
Counter: Walker Zanger
Floors: Alber Arias Hardwood Flooring
Shower hardware: Newport Brass
Lighting: Recessed
Plumbing supplies: Mike Aldred at Ferguson's

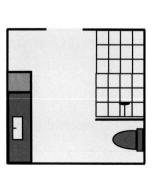

PHOTOGRAPHER: ALISON HAHN

Sublime Comforts

DESIGNER
Nick G. Virgilio,
CKD, CGR
Janco Design
Group, Inc.
236 Crest Court
Bloomingdale, IL 60108
630-529-2487

SPECIAL FEATURES
Dual skylights; matching
birch tub apron; custom
tile design

DIMENSIONS
10' x 14'

PRODUCTS USED
Tile: Florida Tile
Cabinetry: Luxor
Mirrors: Luxor
Sink(s): Kohler
Tub: MTI
Toilet: Kohler
Shower Door: Custom
heavy glass
Shower head:
Delta Select
Sink Faucets:
Delta Select
Shower Faucets:
Delta Select
Vanity Tops: Cambria
Lights: Minka Lavery
Drawer Pulls:
Top Knobs
Accessories:
Allied Brass
Shower:
Cultured Marble

WITH A TRUE APPRECIATION for relaxation and organization, the owners of this suburban Chicago home envisioned converting their cramped, four-bedroom upper level into a roomy, three-bedroom space. The owners hired designer Nick G. Virgilio, CKD, CGR, of Janco Design Group, Inc., to make their dreams a reality.

The project focus was to create a master suite, which would include everything from a walk-in closet with built-in cabinetry to a spacious master bathroom. The challenge of this plan was in meeting all of the homeowners' desires by using only the existing space. After decisions were finalized for the bedroom, attention was then turned to the bathroom. By relocating the existing closet, enough room was created to more than double the size of the existing bathroom. This allowed for the new space to include a 6-foot MTI Whirlpool tub, a 4-foot neo-angle shower base, as well as a double vanity with a tall linen storage cabinet. The linen cabinet conceals a small television with a cable connection, allowing the homeowners to unwind in a pool of comfort in their new whirlpool tub. Installing two overhead skylights created plentiful natural light.

Both the walls and the floor are covered with Florida Tile's porcelain Las Olas collection, with the layout created by the homeowners themselves. In the end, the homeowners are left with a spacious, luxurious ambiance in which they can relax and soak up the comforts of home. «

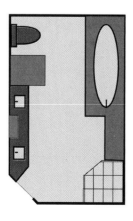

PHOTOGRAPHER: STEVEN PAUL WHITSITT

Breathtaking Views

THIS BATHROOM IS THE RESULT of a complete remodel. Through the process, one of the biggest challenges involved a 100-plus-year-old dresser that belonged to the designer's wife's grandmother. A sink had to be cut into the dresser and plumbing incorporated without affecting the workability of the drawers.

Another challenge was to work the pump on the back side of the Whirlpool so that it circulated water. A catch basin was installed in the back, and a pump was incorporated to circulate the water up to the spout and back into the basin. Blue coloring was added to enhance the effect of the water.

The walls were hand-painted, and careful attention was given to creating cohesive detail throughout the room. The sink-in-dresser was hand-painted and refired. Because the homeowners have five sons, five bluebirds were incorporated into the design to represent the boys.

A slab of Corian matching the Kohler Portrait toilet had to be installed to raise the toilet from 14" to 17". The floor and deck consist of ceramic tile and have the appearance of slate. The installation of electric matting beneath the tile keeps guests warm after relaxing in the whirlpool bath and provides heat for the room. The shutters were custom made to fit the windows so bathers could either have privacy or a viewing of the outdoors. «

DESIGNER
Harlan Theo Heineman
Danny Heinemann &
Son's Plbg. & Htg. Inc.
13980 East Schutt Road
Sardinia, NY 14134
716-496-5037

SPECIAL FEATURES
Hand-painted walls
& fixtures by Victoria
George (Decorative
Arts Studio, Arcade,
NY), working picture
pump, 100-plus-year-old
dresser made into vanity

DIMENSIONS
11' x 10'

PRODUCTS USED
Tile: 12 x 12 in. Earth-
scapes Rain Forest
Cabinetry: Antique
dresser
Mirrors: Antique mirror
Sink(s): Kohler Chenille
countertop lavatory
Tub: Maax Kashmie w/
hydromax II air massage
and back max
Toilet: Kohler Portrait
with French curve seat
Sink Faucets: Delta
Victorian Collection in
Venetian Bronze
Tub: Delta Victorian
Collection Roman Tub
filler w/ hand-held
shower
Heated floors:
Warmly Yours

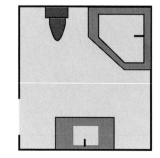

PHOTOGRAPHER: STEVEN WHITSITT

High-Tech High Rise

THE WILSHIRE CORRIDOR IS PERHAPS one of the most desirable locations for those seeking luxurious high-rise living. It's no surprise then that residents of the corridor desire interiors as swanky as their address. So when Nicole Sassaman's colleague Tom Sudinsky opted to remodel his own Wilshire high-rise, he wanted to design a fitting bathroom.

The designer desired a rich, masculine aesthetic. He also wanted to disguise the view of the toilet from the bedroom. His dilemma: how to achieve such tasks without tearing everything out and starting from scratch. To solve the problems, Sudinsky decided to reface his cabinets with walnut and new hardware. He also chose to replace the existing sink faucets with a set by Newport Brass. Sudinsky then placed a custom-crafted walnut shelving unit on top of the counter between the sinks. Inside he housed a plasma TV, as well as other necessities. He hung Ralph Lauren wallpaper on the walls.

To disguise the toilet, Sudinksky removed the bidet from the toilet closet and replaced it with a beautiful antique chest. He placed the toilet to the left of the chest, thus hiding it from view when looking in from the master bedroom. Though hidden, the high-tech toilet boasts a variety of innovative features, including a lid that automatically opens and closes, a seat warmer, and a scent diffuser. «

DESIGNER
Tom Sudinsky

DIMENSIONS
12' x 6'

PRODUCTS USED
Cabinetry: Existing, refaced with walnut
Faucet(s): Newport Brass
Toilet: Toto Neorest
Hardware: Details
Flooring: Wood parquet
Wallcovering: Ralph Lauren Wallpaper

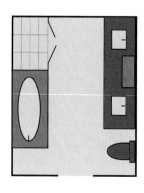

Expanding Space

DUE TO THE GENERALLY LIMITED SPACES IN BATHROOMS, necessity often causes renovations to consist mainly of fixtures and finishes. Such was not the case with this bathroom and walk-in closet.

The space was extremely inefficient. No door existed between the master bedroom and bath; instead, there was an opening with a pair of small closets along the wall. The vanity was crowded along the shortest wall of the room, and too much of the room consisted of open, empty unusable space.

With specific ideas about what he wanted, the client-contracted Brian McGarry, of Kitchen Classics by Custom Crafters, to create his ideal space.

McGarry began the project by dividing the area into two separate rooms to provide a large walk-in closet for the client's extensive wardrobe. This division also served to create a large bath with double vanities and a luxurious shower. A new wall was created to divide the rooms, and pocket doors were installed to connect the new rooms with the bedroom. Additionally, the toilet was moved, the vanities were placed along the new wall, and the old tub became the shower. A custom-reeded glass window was installed to allow clear light into the space while maintaining privacy. Warm Juparana Columbo granite and polished brass fixtures added the final touch of luxury to these newly efficient rooms. «

DESIGNER
Brian McGarry
Kitchen Classics by
Custom Crafters, Inc.
6023 Wilson Blvd.
Arlington, VA 22205
703-532-7000

4000 Howard Ave.
Kensington, MD 20895
301-493-4000

SPECIAL FEATURES
Japarana Columbo
granite; custom-reeded
glass window

DIMENSIONS
10' x 11' (Bath)
7' x 11' (Closet)

PRODUCTS USED
Wall Tile: Juparana
Columbo, Marblex
Cabinetry: Durasupreme,
Maple color ginger
Mirrors: Bel Pre Glass
Sink(s): Kohler
Toilet: Kohler
Shower Door: Custom,
Bel Pre Glass
**Shower Head and
Personal Hand Shower:**
Grohe
Sink Faucets: Grohe
Medicine Cabinets:
Robern
Vanity Tops: Juparana
Columbo slab, Marblex
Drawer Pulls: Allied Brass
Walk-in closet cabinetry:
DuraSupreme

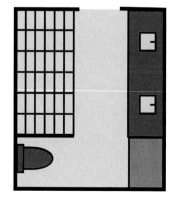

PHOTOGRAPHER: STEVE WHITSITT

Hollywood Regency

O WNER D AVID G RAY desired a classic Hollywood Regency look for his master bath. The existing design, however, was too compartmentalized and dark; the space needed to be opened to allow light from the one window to permeate the room. To solve his dilemma, designer Brian Little removed the existing walls and doorways. This allowed entrants to see light from the window.

To complete his Hollywood Regency aesthetic, Little installed old-fashioned-styled tiles. He then incorporated a claw-foot tub with chrome legs. A custom vanity cabinet and marble counters further enhance the theme. The shower features Tassos marble by Ann Sacks. The medicine cabinets by Kohler include electrical outlets on the inside, which allows Gray to keep items such as his razor neatly placed out of sight.

When creating a similar design for your own bath, Nicole Sassaman advises applying these same inventive solutions. If marble may put your remodeling budget in the red, consider a solid surface such as Silestone or CaesarStone. You can also purchase an antique claw-foot tub and resurface it by reapplying porcelain. The finished results will be a bath befitting of Hollywood glam. «

DESIGNER
Brian Little

DIMENSIONS
15' x 6'6"

PRODUCTS USED
Marble: Ann Sacks
Vanity cabinet: Custom
Medicine chests: Kohler
Sink(s): Kohler
Faucet(s): Kohler
Tub: Sunrise Specialty
Vanity tops:
Carrera marble
Lighting: Restoration
Hardware
Fixtures: Kohler

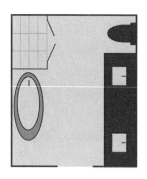

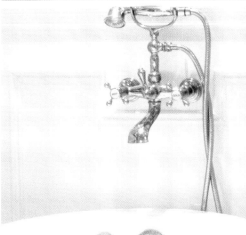

PHOTOGRAPHER: ALISON HAHN

Hillside Retreat

LOCATED IN SWANKY HASLAM TERRACE in Los Angeles, California, this house had a bathroom that was not only short on space but even shorter on substance. The homeowners desired big style for their small bath. To help them realize their dreams, they worked with designer Tom Sudinsky and contractor Navarro Construction.

To help make the most of the confined area, Sudinsky chose to suspend the bathroom mirror from the ceiling directly in front of the window. This configuration opened up the area in front of the shower, where Sudinsky placed the sink. Behind the door he installed a custom-built, shallow shelf and cabinet. The unit is designed to accommodate towels and bathroom necessities. He placed the toilet opposite the shelf.

Inside the shower, Sudinsky opted to use a thin, small white subway tile. The tile assisted in maintaining an open, linear design. He then paired the shower with a seamless shower door. The effect is a tight-on-size bathroom that boasts a variety of high-style design elements. «

DESIGNER
Tom Sudinsky

DIMENSIONS
6'6" x 4'6"

PRODUCTS USED
Cabinetry: Custom cherry from Roelke Woodworking
Floors: Cork by Wicander
Countertops: CaesarStone
Mirrors: Custom
Sink(s): Kohler
Faucet(s): Hansgrohe
Toilet: Toto
Wall covering: Clarence House

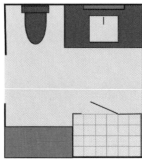

PHOTOGRAPHER: ALISON HAHN

Vintage Paradise

A LUXURIOUS KOHLER VINTAGE SOAKING TUB and a breathtaking view create the focal point for this exquisite bathroom designed by Denise Quade, of Bella Domicile, Inc. Known for her beautiful kitchen and bath designs, Quade was chosen to work with the homeowners and employ her expertise to achieve the desired results. In the end, the project was a stunning success.

His and her vanities designed with period style and beaded inset cherry cabinets sit at the entry to this relaxing retreat, providing elegant appeal. The his-and-her theme is also carried through to the separate linen cabinets and makeup area. Additionally, Giallo Veneziano granite countertops complete with unique backsplashes work to enhance the ambiance.

A spacious walk-in shower and segregated toilet area provide functionality and style. Vaulted ceilings enhanced by cherry beams and a gorgeous picture window add to the unique shape of the room and contribute to the theme of the space. Crowned by an enchanting Princella crystal chandelier and crystal sconces lighting the vanities, this bathroom is nothing short of an elegant retreat. «

DESIGNER
Denise Quade, CKD
Bella Domicile, Inc.
6210 Nesbitt Road
Madison, WI 53719
608-271-8241

SPECIAL FEATURES
His and her vanities; makeup table; soaking tub; walk-in shower; natural stone countertops

DIMENSIONS
16' x 23'

PRODUCTS USED
Cabinetry: Dutch Made Radcliffe door style, beaded inset, cherry
Sink(s): Kohler
Tub: Kohler Vintage
Toilet: Kohler
Vanity Tops: Giallo Veneziano granite
Lights: Princella Crystal chandelier
Drawer Pulls: Richeleau

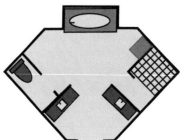

A Bachelor Pad

DESIGNER
Rochelle Kalisch
Regency Kitchens Inc.
4204 14th Avenue
Brooklyn, NY 11219
718-435-4266

204 E. 77th St., Ste. 1E
New York, NY 10021
212-517-8707

SPECIAL FEATURES
Custom curved
mahogany cabinets;
onyx vanity top and
slab on floor; charcoal
Turkish marble.

DIMENSIONS
5' x 9'

PRODUCTS USED
Tile: Marble "Foliage"
onyx- International
Stone & Accessories
Cabinetry: Mahogany
– Regency Kitchens
Mirrors: Mirrored
medicine cabinet-
Regency Kitchens
Sink(s):
Kohler-K2200 (Meriot)
Toilet: Kohler K3434
(Meriot)
Showerdoor:
Duschqueen
Showerhead:
Chicago Faucet
Sink Faucets: Gemini
Shower Faucets:
Chicago Faucet
Vanity Tops: Onyx-
International Stone &
Accessories
Lighting: recessed
lighting-Lightolier

THE ENCLOSED BATHROOM was designed for a New York City penthouse condo recently purchased by a young bachelor stockbroker. Although the apartment is in a prestigious neighborhood, the space appeared long, narrow, and boring.

When the client contacted Rochelle Kalisch, of Regency Kitchens Inc., to help in the redesign, her initial reaction was to create a more spacious feeling and a more dramatic space. This was in accord with the homeowner's wish for a "masculine" space with drama and excitement. Taking that into account, Kalisch chose to work with an exciting variety of materials and shapes. A dark toilet and light onyx flooring and countertops were selected, a stark and imposing contrast. The placement of marble tile and onyx slabs helps to create a separate powder-room effect; so does the shallow tall wall between the shower/toilet and the vanity.

In order to create the spacious and dramatic effect in the powder area, custom curved cabinetry was designed with plenty of storage space. Polished brass fixtures and a curved onyx slab for a countertop adds to the airy feel. A built-in medicine cabinet above this countertop gives a clean, streamlined look. The window was enlarged and fitted with special privacy glass.

The combination of curved cabinetry and onyx slab together with the grid pattern of marble tiles creates a striking and masculine high-tech atmosphere. «

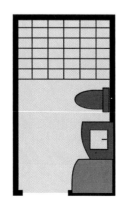

PHOTOGRAPHER: STEVEN PAUL WHITSITT

Personal Retreat

THE OWNERS of this lovely home love to spend extended time in the bathroom showering and retreating from the world. Among their many requests were a linen closet for storing towels and other sundries, as well as two sinks and knee space for applying makeup and hair drying. With limited space available, the industrial designer, Ellen Shelly, faced some challenges. As this remodel began taking shape, Shelly was asked to plan a cozy space that was neither masculine nor feminine but a warm, inviting environment.

Shelly incorporated a way to include the linen closets on either side of the vanity and provide a space for a custom-made stool. Leaving the counter at the same level and not dropping it down to desk height allowed the space to seem larger and made it more efficient. The client needed additional drawer storage that could not be accommodated within the vanity area, so Shelly installed the small accessory chest of drawers.

The fireplace was placed across from the Jacuzzi whirlpool, giving not only a heat source but also adding tremendous ambience to the room.

The custom-stained glazed cabinetry also added to the space. Shelly's choice of Kohler sinks and faucets provided a beautiful complement to the marble tops and whirlpool. Overall, the clients received a striking, warm space that allows them to enjoy everything they desired. «

DESIGNER
Ellen Shelly
Shelly Design, Inc.
709 Mt. Moriah Drive,
Suite 106
Cincinnati, OH 45245
513-752-1606

SPECIAL FEATURES
Special finish; stain glaze; makeup area; linen storage and decorative dresser for additional storage.

DIMENSIONS
12'9" x 8'

PRODUCTS USED
Cabinetry: Recker Custom Woodworks
Flooring: Discontinued Tile
Countertops: Statuary White Marble with Eased Edge
Mirrors: Basco
Sink: Kohler
Faucet: Kohler Revival
Whirlpool: Jacuzzi
Toilet: Kohler (Not Shown)
Shower Door: Basco
Drawer Pulls: Top Knobs

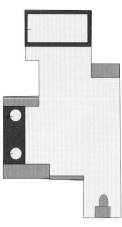

Vintage Retreat

THE HOMEOWNERS LOVED THE LATE-1800S MANSION they'd bought in a Chicago suburb, but they knew the bathroom was outdated. Cosmetic changes by the previous owner had not been successful in keeping with the character of the home. The clients wanted a retreat, with their bathroom, bedroom, and closets complementing one another.

They called Gary Lichlyter, of Lemont Kitchen & Bath, to help them create a luxury master suite befitting their elegant home. He had worked with them on a previous residence, and they were confident that he could turn their dreams into reality.

Lichlyter began with the elements that would remain: a built-in mirror with lots of character and a separate water-closet area for privacy. Utilizing space from an adjacent closet, he gained room for a two-person shower. Multiple shower heads make the spa experience available every day. Pink rose marble perfectly complements the rich cherry-wood cabinetry. Polished chrome period-style faucetry and towel bars—and Kohler's Portrait Series fixtures—suit the style and age of the home. The existing radiant steam-heat system was rerouted to warm the floor tiles.

The homeowner as well as interior designer Charlyn Burrows, of C.B. Interiors, chose pinks, peaches, and creams to set the tone of the room. Crystal hardware, crystal lighting, and beveled-glass mirrors add an elegant touch.

DESIGNER
Gary A. Lichlyter
Lemont Kitchen &
Bath, Inc.
106 Stephen St
Lemont, IL 60439
630-257-8144

SPECIAL FEATURES
Two-person shower
with multi-shower
heads including a "rain"
showerhead; period
faucetry; marble vanity
top; whirlpool deck; and
shower surround.

DIMENSIONS
10' x 19' bathroom
14' x 13' dressing room

PRODUCTS USED
Tile: Ceramic
Cabinetry: Jay Rambo
Whirlpool Tub: Kohler
Vanity tops: Pink Rose
Marble
Sink(s): Kohler
undermount
Toilet: Kohler
Showerhead: Barwil
Sink Faucets: SoHo
Shower Faucets: Barwil
Hardware: Crystal

PHOTOGRAPHER: STOCKER PHOTOGRAPHY

To The Front

WHEN IT WAS TIME TO REMODEL THEIR MASTER SUITE, the homeowners contacted Karen Bieszczak, CKD, of Bzak Design Group, to guide their project. Working with Ellen Shelly, of Shelly Design, Bieszczak surveyed the situation and made a recommendation: moving the master bath toward the front would provide beneficial opportunities. The designers set out to convince their clients of the wisdom in that plan, pointing out the improved layout that would be possible.

Due to the windows that were lower than the proposed counter height, the bath was configured in an L-shaped space that ultimately enhanced the private features of the twin vanities and toilet area.

His taller vanity and storage rack installed on the door of the tall linen cabinet optimized his storage needs. The elegance of her vanity is seen in the hutch-style cabinets, sconces, and mirror with beaded backdrop.

Hawaiian green granite visually links the two vanities. Hardwood floors give a much-needed warmth to the space. The arch valance details are repeated at the cozy niche of the whirlpool.

The finished master suite, including the bath, is comfortable and attractive with all the amenities. The homeowners are delighted that they "came forward" with their beautiful bath. «

DESIGNER
Karen A. Bieszczak, CKD
Bzak Design Group
614 Wooster Pike, Suite 3
Terrace Park, OH 45174
513-831-3155

SPECIAL FEATURES
Privacy feature of
his and her vanities;
whirlpool niche.

DIMENSIONS
10' x 14'

PRODUCTS USED
Tile: Crossville
Cabinetry: Cabinets by Nichols
Mirrors: By Owner
Sink(s): Kohler
Sink Faucets: Kohler
Tub: Kohler
Toilet: Kohler
Shower Door: Basco
Showerhead: Kohler
Shower Faucets: Kohler
Vanity Tops: Hawaiian Green Granite
Lights: By Owner
Plumbing Supplies: Kohler
Drawer Pulls: Bona Decorative Hardware

PHOTOGRAPHER: DAVID STEINBRUNNER

Hotel Luxury

THIS HOMEOWNER LIKED HIS HASSLE-FREE CONDOMINIUM in an upscale golf-course community but wanted to inject his own style into the plans.

The client, who travels extensively, wanted the amenities of fine hotels: a television, steam unit, large shower, and lots of marble. He got all that, plus a hand-carved Italian marble fireplace, in a space that was small and had no window.

Haskell Matheny reconfigured the hallway, existing bath, and closets into a classic octagon, with the master closet at one end. With no window for a focus over the tub, he placed mirrors in the whirlpool alcove and added a mirrored display case. One custom-designed etched-glass door leads to the water closet, its mate to the walk-in shower and steam unit.

Above the fireplace is a hidden 27-inch television. Also tucked away is a pair of medicine cabinets. Custom-designed butterfly mahogany chests flank the fireplace, each with a black-and-gold marble counter, gold leaf accents, and gold-plated fixtures.

Polished marble on the floors and walls underscores the room's elegance. Lining the walls is a custom mirrored chair rail inlaid with a gold Greek key design. Haskell deliberately chose highly polished, reflective surfaces on every item to bring richness and sparkle into this luxurious master suite.

Now this homeowner has what he considers the ultimate luxurious bath right in his own home. «

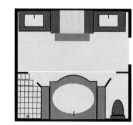

DESIGNER
Haskell R. Matheny
Haskell Interiors, LLC.
85 1st Street N.E.
Cleveland, TN 37311
423-472-6409

SPECIAL FEATURES
Hand-carved marble fireplace; hidden T.V. above mantel; gold-leaf mirrored greek key chair rail; display niche; custom engraved shower and water closet doors; hidden medicine cabinets; custom butterfly mahogany vanities

DIMENSIONS
13' x 16'

PRODUCTS USED
Cabinetry: High Style Kitchens
Tile: Marble – Rossa Verona
Mirrors: Decorative Crafts
Sink(s): Porcher
Tub: Ultra
Toilet: Kohler
Shower Door: Custom glass engraving
Showerhead: Grohe
Sink Faucets: Sigma
Vanity Tops: Marble – Black & Gold Potoro
Lighting: Metropolitan
Mantel: Architectural Accents
Other: Molding: Outwater Plastics

PHOTOGRAPHER: STEPHEN GREENFIELD

Bye-Bye Boring

The original bathroom was designed in the 1960s for a master suite in a traditional Brooklyn brownstone. It was a fairly spacious room but lacked style and personality. In short, it was boring.

The clients wanted an ultimately comfortable space filled with the latest bathroom gadgets, and accommodating to their lifestyle. Taking this into account, Rochelle Kalisch, CKD, chose to work with a traditional selection of materials but used an angled composition for floor tiles, dropped ceiling, and vanity cabinetry to create drama. She selected dark-green marble tiles for the walls, floor, and vanity top, and pure-white fixtures and decorative ceramic border around the mirror. Dark-cherry cabinetry and crown molding and polished-brass faucets and hand shower create a stark and imposing contrast. In order to continue the drama in the vanity area, Kalisch designed custom angled cabinetry with polished-brass hardware that allow for plenty of storage and a makeup desk. A built-in medicine cabinet was installed in the angled wall behind the sink vanity cabinet.

The clients wanted a full-size whirlpool and Jacuzzi shower unit, and the designer was able to accommodate those in the creation of this beautiful room.

In the end, the homeowners were left with a grand 21st-century addition to their master suite. «

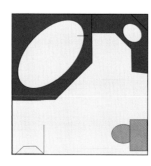

DESIGNER
Rochelle Kalisch, CKD
Regency Kitchens
204 E. 77th St.
New York, NY 10021
212-517-8707

4204 14th Ave.
Brooklyn, NY 11219
718-435-4266

SPECIAL FEATURES
Angled composition of whirlpool platform; cabinetry and dropped ceiling create drama; combination of stark-white tiles and fixtures, dark-green marble with white veins, cherry wood furniture and brass accents create glamour

DIMENSIONS
10'6" x 10'6"

PRODUCTS USED
Tile: Country Floor
Cabinetry: Regency Kitchens
Mirrors: Regency Kitchens
Sink(s): Kohler K2210
Tub: Kohler K1348
Toilet: Kohler K3434
Shower: Jacuzzi J-90
Showerhead: Jado
Sink Faucets: Jado
Shower Faucets: Jado
Vanity Tops: Green marble

PHOTOGRAPHER: OLEG MARSH

Bye-Bye Blue

WE'VE ALL SEEN the old American Standard blue bathroom. At one time, it seemed it was in every other house, including that of this Illinois homeowner.

She wanted a special place to pamper herself, and while blue may be soothing, the hue in this room was tired, and the bath was badly in need of an update. It was anything, but special.

Working with Terry Hansen, of Hansen's Remodeling in Downers Grove, Ill., Damian Slabosz, of Beauty Craft, headed up the project, which included replacing the vanity, countertops, sink, toilet, floor and a one-piece shower stall. Basically, they created the room from scratch.

A little investigation revealed some unused attic space, which they were able to capitalize on, adding a pair of octagon windows to let in lots of natural light, which was supplemented with recessed can lights and a light on the ceiling fan.

Softer colors took over—almond tile on the floor and wainscot, peach plumbing fixtures and Corian tub surround, a deep-cherry stain with a polished gloss finish on the cabinetry—but blue wasn't banished entirely. The designer used it as an accent in the rope-style tile trim, accents in the floor, and a custom Corian chair rail. Solid-brass faucets and a lighted mirror over the toilet lend an elegant touch. The result is a bath with a fresh, modern look and more light to boot. «

DESIGNER
Damian J. Slabosz
Beauty Craft Inc. Designs
By Damian
213 E. Ogden Ave.
Westmont, IL 60559
630-654-2552

SPECIAL FEATURES
Polished cherry cabinets; piano key soap dish; utilized attic space for natural sunlight

DIMENSIONS
5' x 12'

PRODUCTS USED
Tile: American Olean
Cabinetry: Designs by Damian, Estate door style
Mirrors: Basco
Sink(s): American Standard, Ellise Petite pedestal
Tub: American Standard, Americast Princeton
Toilet: American Standard, Lexington
Shower Door: Basco frameless
Showerhead: Artistic Brass
Sink Faucets: Artistic Brass
Shower Faucets: Artistic Brass
Vanity Tops: DuPont Corian
Lights: Halo

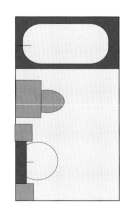

PHOTOGRAPHER: STEVE WHITSIT

Country Warmth

THIS SMALL BATHROOM contained a standard-issue toilet, vanity, and tub. In its place, the client desired an upscale guest bath that would also contain a larger whirlpool tub. To accomplish this, Mary Maier Galloway, CKD, of Kitchen Classics by Custom Crafters, expanded the bath space into an adjacent coat closet, gaining an additional 6 feet. The extra room easily allowed her to install a large whirlpool tub.

The ambiance of the bath is attained with aged, texturally rich tumbled Crema Marfil tile and Emperador tile, which are contrasted with the smooth lines of the biscuit-colored fixtures and dark chocolate-stained vanity cabinet.

The client's trip to Tuscany served as inspiration for the bath's décor. Every element of the design beautifully captures the romance of the region—from the branching arms of a lemon tree in the recess above the tub to the tranquil farm scene on the opposite wall.

While aware of the ambience the client desired, Galloway was also concerned about safety of lighting combined with water. As this room would have only a bathtub, she wanted to ensure the client only had lighting that was safe. She chose to light the bath with MR16's, and the additional down light over the tub is of U.L.-rated waterproof construction. The bath provides a rich retreat for its owners and a beautifully appointed guest bath. «

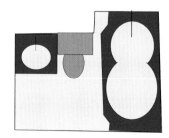

DESIGNER
Kitchen Classics by Custom Crafters, Inc.
6023 Wilson Blvd.
Arlington, VA 22205
703-532-7000

SPECIAL FEATURES
Inspired by client's trip to Tuscany. Hand painted tiles represent lemon tree and view of Tuscan country side

DIMENSIONS
7' x 7'6''

PRODUCTS USED
Tile: Tumbled Crema Marfil and Emperador Marble Tile
Cabinetry: Kohler
Mirrors: Pottery Barn
Sink: Kohler
Tub: Jacuzzi, Merano Whirlpool with Inline Heater and Neck Jets
Toilet: Kohler
Sink Faucets: F.V., Temple Design Wall Mount, Chrome
Tub Filler: Kohler, Souris, Wallmount Sheet Flow
Lighting: Task, Halogen Recessed Directional Fixtures
Tile Artist/Muralist: Pat Bergeron

Comfort Zone

The architect's original blueprints were altered, and the original bathroom, together with a small closet, became the new space for the master bath in this new home. The new homeowners wanted a large spa-like bathroom reminiscent of ancient Rome or Greece. Designer Amir Ilin, of Küche+Cucina, loved the idea and started the research for the project.

Custom sandblasted antique glass tiles were selected as an accent for the antique limestone floor. Ilin added the matching glass mosaic tile for the shower walls, ceiling and the border around the room. A historic Roman design was adapted to create the custom handmade mosaic on the shower wall.

"Carefully broken" slabs were used for the rest of the walls and for the shower seat. A limestone half-column was placed inside the shower to support the seat. Handmade solid stone bathroom sinks, made by Minds Eye, were installed on both vanities.

Ilin designed the cabinetry and tub surroundings to blend with the natural colors of the stone and blend with the old world styling. Toscan brass finish was selected for this steam shower and the rest of the bathroom fixtures.

Well-known artist Joe Brown was commissioned to paint the walls and complete the scenery of the master bath, which is now the homeowner's new comfort zone. «

DESIGNER
Amir Ilin
Küche+Cucina
489 Route 17 South
Paramus, NJ 07652
201-261-5221

SPECIAL FEATURES
Hand selected, bookmatched rotary sliced white birch veneers with radiused end panels.

DIMENSIONS
18' x 12'

PRODUCTS USED
Tile: Antiqued Limestone Floors. Cabinetry: Küche+Cucina
Custom Sink: Handmade Solid Stone
Tub: Jacuzzi
Toilet: Kohler
Shower Door: Custom Showerhead, Sink and Shower Faucets: Rohl Toscan Brass
Vanity Tops: Travertine Plumbing Supplies: Rohl
Drawer Pulls: Omnia
Steam Shower: Mr. Steam
Custom Mosaic: En 'Stone
Mural: Joe Brown

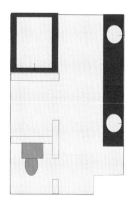

PHOTOGRAPHER: MARK BALZARETTE

Spaciously Cozy

THESE HOMEOWNERS WERE HAPPY to have a spacious bathroom, but they also wanted the room to feel intimate and cozy. This left designer Betsy House, of Kitchen & Bath Designs, and builder/designer Hayward Gatch with the job of dividing the space in such a way that would make the room appear both attractive and functional. Additionally, the designers were tasked with incorporating the same nautical flare in the bath as they had in the family's kitchen.

To fully develop the nautical theme, the designers used wood counters, a wood ceiling, and varnished wood details. They also chose to incorporate a variety of special features to set the room apart from other baths. For example, an old boat hatchway in the ceiling leads to the family's air unit; this is the perfect example of a functional piece turned decorative.

French doors open into this bath and align with an archway that encompasses his and her vanity stations. A beautiful window seat located below the arch allows the homeowners a cozy place to sit, rest, and retreat from the demands of busy days. The finished project is a delightful respite from the stresses of everyday life. «

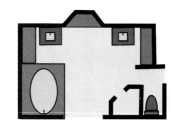

DESIGNER
Betsy House
Kitchen & Bath Designs,
LLC by Betsy House
11 Heritage Drive
Stonington, CT 06378
860-535-4982

SPECIAL FEATURES
Chamfered posts,
arches; window seat; his
and her vanity stations;
arched mahogany
medicine cabinets;
antique heart-pine tub
deck and floor; wainscot
panels on walls; linen
closet

DIMENSIONS
15' x 10'

PRODUCTS USED
Flooring:
Antique heart pine
**Cabinetry and medicine
cabinets:** Paul Deschenes
& Co., Inc.
Countertops: Smith &
Turbana antique heart
pine
Sink: St. Thomas
Creations console tables
Faucets: Newport brass
Toilet: Kohler
Shower Door: Kohler Neo
Angle unit with steam
shower
Drawer Pulls: Crown City
cut crystal knobs

PHOTOGRAPHER: OLSON PHOTOGRAPHIC (JOHN AND CASSIDY OLSON)

Design on a Dime

PRIOR TO ITS REMODEL, this basic bath sat empty most days of the month. Once Alice Anna Cloar, of The Kitchen Gallery, got her hands on the space, she transformed the room into a luxurious, spacious environment that begs daily use. The redesigned bath promotes relaxation and provides the homeowners with the simple pleasure of indulging in a luxurious shower at the end of a long day.

Though these Tennessee homeowners desired a personal retreat, they were on a strict budget. Fully aware of this stipulation, Cloar worked to keep the selected items within a moderate price range. Additional challenges included the small size of the room and the existence of a partition separating the tub from the vanity. In answer, Cloar replaced the tub with a shower and removed the partition to make the room appear larger.

The designer enlarged the shower to include body sprays, proper lighting, shelf space, a seating area, and ventilation. In an effort to visually enlarge the space, she selected a frameless glass shower enclosure and door. A furniture vanity, two sinks, granite countertops, and wall storage units complete the room. The final result is a budget-friendly at-home retreat. «

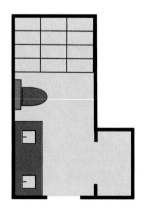

DESIGNER
Alice Anna Cloar
The Kitchen Gallery
1034 Woodland Ave.
Knoxville, TN 37917
865-524-3457

DESIGN FEATURES
Custom 36" base cabinets; self-closing drawers; large shower with built-in bench

DIMENSIONS
5' x 14'

PRODUCTS USED
Tile: Winco; Pietra Art; Giallo
Cabinetry: Holiday
Mirrors: American Lighting
Sinks: Ferguson's; Kohler
Shower: Tile
Toilet: Ferguson's
Shower Door: Greg Kurtz custom mirror, glass
Vanity Tops: Marble Works granite
Lights: American Lighting, Canterbury Collection
Plumbing Supplies: Ferguson's; Delta
Drawer Pulls: Top Knobs
Wallcovering: Winco tile; Benjamin Moore paint

Tudor Beauty

NEWLY MARRIED AND READY to make their house a home, this Wisconsin couple had dreams to envelope their master bath in classic English Tudor character, charm, and grace. The homeowners tapped the expertise of Bella Domicile designer Denise Quade for the total redo, which transformed the space from ordinary to extraordinary.

Quade's biggest challenge: The homeowners knew exactly how they wanted the room to look, so the designer had to translate their abstract ideas into a concrete creation. A passing glance at this haven is proof that Quade successfully accomplished the task.

Hand-carved onlays and intricate detailing sweep elegantly around the luxurious room; sumptuous medallion-encrusted mosaics mesh tastefully with the imported floor tile and stone countertop. A toilet room and bidet provide privacy, while a makeup counter under the window separates his and her vanities. The homeowner also needed a spot to store her oversized jewelry chest and to showcase her extensive collection of decorative perfume bottles, so Quade made sure to set aside ample space for all the baubles and beads. The huge walk-in closet contains one additional perk: lots of room to stow plenty of shoes!

With its vibrant vintage style and delightful, personalized décor, this English Tudor-inspired master bath is an American masterpiece. «

DESIGNER
Denise Quade, CKD
Bella Domicile Inc.
6210 Nesbitt Rd.
Madison, WI 53719
608-271-8241

SPECIAL FEATURES
English Tudor styling;
hand-carved onlays;
toilet plus bidet; his and
her vanities

DIMENSIONS
21' x 30'

PRODUCTS USED
Cabinetry: DutchMade
Beaded Inset, mitred
Florentine door style
Sinks: Undermount
Vanity: 3cm Violetta
Natural Stone

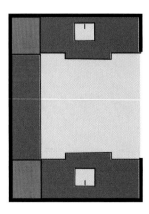

PHOTOGRAPHER: STEVEN PAUL WHITSITT

The Natural Way

Tʜᴇꜱᴇ ᴇᴍᴘᴛʏ-ɴᴇꜱᴛᴇʀꜱ built their near-perfect home years earlier, complete with a spacious master bedroom on the first floor. The master bath, however, fell far short of luxurious. An addition to the existing bath solved the spatial problem and provided much-needed closet space, and his and her vanities added a convenient and attractive luxury. However, the challenge of transforming the space into a dream design still remained.

The homeowners had a vision of an Old World style using natural materials. To create the color palette and guide them through the selections, they engaged decorator Kathleen Penney—who enlisted Michael Clements, of Whole House Cabinetry, Inc.—to design the perfect cabinetry to complete the look. A custom stain and glaze on raised-panel doors and arched valances provided strong furniture elements while keeping a light ambiance. Marble was selected for the floors and countertops.

Together, Penney and Clements created a master bath that matches the timeless décor of the rest of the home, and the clients are delighted that their beloved home is now a welcome retreat. «

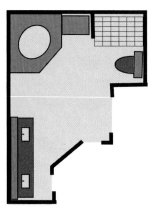

DESIGNER
Michael Clements
Whole House
Cabinetry, Inc.
2948 Conestoga Rd.
Glenmoore, PA 19343
610-459-4428

SPECIAL FEATURES
Spacious floor plan; his and her vanities; unique custom cabinetry

DIMENSIONS
25' x 18'

PRODUCTS USED
Cabinetry: Custom Bertch
Flooring: Tumbled marble
Countertops: Marble
Sinks: Kohler
Faucets: Kohler
Mirrors: Custom
Toilet: Kohler
Shower Door: Custom
Vanity Tops: Marble
Plumbing Supplies: Kohler
Drawer Pulls: Top Knobs
Tub: Kohler

PHOTOGRAPHER: STEVEN PAUL WHITSITT

A Sweet Suite

FINDING THE RIGHT HOME can be a daunting task, especially in an area known for its bland, safe designs. When the owners of this 4-year-old Naperville, Illinois, home first entered this house, they fell in love. After seeing the poorly designed builder-grade master bathroom, though, they had to make a decision: keep searching or purchase and remodel? They purchased, and sought the expertise of a designer who could transform their space into an awe-inspiring bath.

Jessica A. Gomes, of the Casa Bella Design Center, devised a plan to overcome the many challenges of the space. By gutting the entire bathroom, she was able to redesign the layout, focusing first on a large closet and smaller secondary closet. Both were necessities for her clients' storage needs. Gomes also designed a custom vanity area with warm-maple floating cabinets, an elevated tub surrounded by unique textured tile, and a large shower area with body sprays and a frameless glass enclosure.

To unify the three areas, Gomes placed a dark, horizontal accent border that encompasses the room and blends with the countertop. She continued this emphasis by installing horizontal cabinet hardware and light fixtures. The thoughtful layout and unique design details created a master bath worthy of its charming home. «

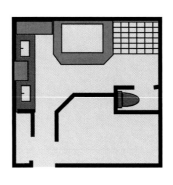

DESIGNER
Jessica A. Gomes
Casa Bella Design Center
15 W. Jefferson Ave.,
Suite 103
Naperville, IL 60540
630-718-1440

SPECIAL FEATURES
Custom-designed
floating cabinets;
frameless glass
shower enclosure;
contemporary plumbing
fixtures; designer
lighting

DIMENSIONS
18' x 17'

PRODUCTS USED
Tile: Rain Forest Earth
with Corian insert
border
Cabinetry: Jay Rambo
Mirrors:
Custom Fit Mirrors
Sinks: Kohler
Tub: Existing
Toilet: Existing
Shower door: Custom
frameless enclosure
Vanity tops: Corian
Lights: Ginger
Plumbing supplies:
Aquadis; Grohe; Moen
Drawer pulls: Top Knobs
Bath accessories: Moen

A Bather's Delight

WHEN THESE EMPTY-NEST HOMEOWNERS returned from their most recent trip to Italy, they desired to re-create the tranquility of the Old World in their home. Long-time aficionados of luxurious bathing, their wish list contained several items.

Jill Ellis, of Colorado Kitchen Designs, LLC in Denver, Colorado, together with Tom Owens, of Creative Remodeling, worked with the clients to assist them in realizing their ideal bath suite. An unused bedroom provided the majority of space, and an existing window became the focal point for the Jetta tub. A new leaded-glass window with custom design allows beautiful light to dance across the room. The Wood Harbor cherry cabinetry is replete with storage options. Additional storage is created with the decorative turnposts, which pull out and provide space for toiletries. The wall cabinet at the head of the tub is not only a handy place to store towels, but it also helps to create a cozy niche feel. Pullout drawers stock bath goodies and matches for candles.

A delightful two-way gas fireplace sits next to the large shower and lends warmth to this opulent space. The fireplace also separates the bath from the master bedroom. With this Old World-inspired bath, these contented homeowners no longer must jet to Italy to bask in European beauty. «

DESIGNER
Jill Ellis
Colorado Kitchen
Designs, LLC
123 Cook St., Suite 101
Denver, CO 80206
303-321-4410

SPECIAL FEATURES
Ample storage for toiletries with pull-out posts and small drawers by tub

DIMENSIONS
13' x 13'

PRODUCTS USED
Tile: Capco ceramic tile
Cabinetry:
Wood Harbor Cabinetry
Mirrors:
Wood Harbor Cabinetry
Sinks:
American Standard
Tub: Jetta Whirlpool
Shower Door:
European frameless
Vanity Tops: Juperana
Caruelus granite
Drawer Pulls: Top Knobs
Faucet: Mico
Fireplace: Heat-n-Glo
Leaded Glass:
Scottish Glass
Windows:
Pella Designer Line

PHOTOGRAPHER: PHILIP WEGENER PHOTOGRAPHY

Renewed Restoration

WISHING TO RESTORE THE VINTAGE FEELING to this 1940s English Tudor purchased from her parents, these homeowners enlisted the design services of Nick Virgilio, of Kitchens & Baths by Janco, to return their small bath to its original '40s styling.

Originally remodeled by her father in 1972, the bath was set under the steep roof line of the Tudor-style gable above the front entry door, limiting its size to only 5x5 feet. There was also no natural light coming into the room due to the elimination of the original window during its last remodel. Virgilio solved these problems by relocating the right wall 30 inches outward and adding a vaulted ceiling, thereby increasing floor space as well as volume. This newly gained space was a perfect spot for the new claw-foot tub, while the space vacated by the former tub was used for a new mosaic tile shower and heavy glass enclosure. A new window in the old opening was now at the end of an 8-foot-long aisle down the center of the room. The 11-foot-high ceiling and new skylight help to give the room a larger, brighter feel.

The vintage-style pedestal lavatory and toilet, complementing chrome fixtures, custom birch cabinetry, and a unique mosaic floor design combine beautifully to create a historic style of days gone by. It is now what the homeowners refer to as "their favorite room in the house." «

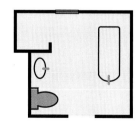

DESIGNER
Nick G. **Virgilio**
Kitchens & Baths by
Janco
236 Crest Ct.
Bloomingdale, IL 60108
630-529-2487

SPECIAL FEATURES
Intricate mosaic floor and wall tile; vaulted ceiling; plant ledge and skylight; claw-foot tub.

DIMENSIONS
8' x 8'

PRODUCTS USED
Tile: Hexagon Mosaic (imported)
Cabinetry & Mirrors: Regency Custom Woodworking
Sinks: Barclay Julia
Tub: Claw-foot
Toilet: Barclay, Julia Toilet
Shower Door: Custom
Showerhead, Sink & Shower Faucets: Delta
Lights: Recessed
Plumbing Supplies: Sunrise Specialties.

Victorian Vintage

WHEN THE OWNERS OF THIS CENTURY-OLD **V**ICTORIAN HOME decided to update their inadequate, structurally damaged bathroom, they wanted to maintain the authentic style of the home, but yearned for a luxurious bathroom with modern conveniences.

Realizing a complete remodel was in order, they enlisted the assistance of professional designer Rebecca Gullion Lindquist, of Lindquist & Co., to magically transform an old 8x10-foot bathroom into a redesigned masterpiece. Because the existing toilet, windows and door could not be moved, Lindquist borrowed 24 inches of space from an adjacent walk-in bedroom closet. Tall storage for linens and a small medicine cabinet were created by recessing into the wall cavities between the framing studs.

An old radiator, located under the windows, was eliminated, creating space for a new whirlpool tub. A large walk-in shower now stands in the space of the former unsafe, inadequately sized claw-foot tub.

Materials reflective of the Victorian era were utilized throughout this space. The 3x6-inch wall tiles used as wainscoting and the two-tone white color scheme are reflective of baths from the early 1900s. The 1-inch hexagonal floor tile matches the tile removed from the old space. The careful details of the moldings, graceful corbels, lead crystal hardware, and white porcelain-and-chrome faucetry and accessories combine to create a bathroom that is bright and fresh. «

DESIGNER
Rebecca Gullion
Lindquist, CKD, CBD,
Lindquist and Company
926 E. 4th St.
Duluth, MN 55805
218-728-5171

SPECIAL FEATURES
Walk-in shower; 5½-foot whirlpool tub; Dupont Corian to ps; custom-designed dressing table.

DIMENSIONS
10' x 10'

PRODUCTS USED
Floors: American Olean
Shower Walls & Ceiling, Wainscot & Tub Platform: Nemo Lanka
Cabinetry: Lindquist Signature by Jay Rambo
Mirrors: Custom
Sink: Dupont Corian
Tub: Kohler
Toilet: Kohler Portrait
Showerhead, Sink & Shower Faucets: Moen
Vanity Tops: Dupont Corian
Lights: Recessed Incandescent, Drawer Pulls: Cliffside, In-floor Heat by Domotek
Tub Fittings: Moen

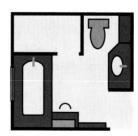

Old World Inspiration

DESIRING A SOOTHING BLEND of "Floridian" ambiance and Old World appeal, these homeowners also wanted to "fill their bathroom's space" by visually bringing down the ceiling and adding creative ledges with height differentials to accommodate both husband and wife.

Professional designer Mike Teipen, of Kitchens by Teipen, and Interior Designer Ray Turner took on this challenge by creating the dream bathroom that these homeowners longed for. Teipen's design solutions included a non-traditional placement of the vanity, bathing, and toilet areas to enhance the elegance of the room. The shower is a custom walk-in area totally covered with Travertine marble. The toilet area is enclosed with functional storage above. The back-to-back his and her vanities extend into the room with custom-designed, multi-curved end pieces, sharing a common custom-made lighted mirror with a decorative sandblasted border.

To visually enhance the room, columns and arches were placed at the entrance to the master bedroom and at the entrance to the master bath. Shelves extending out from the vanity wall provide the proper distance for task lighting below and indirect lighting above.

Accessories including a family urn, an heirloom antique art-deco light fixture, an Oriental rug, and alabaster sconces complete the theme, creating a luxuriously royal bathroom that would have made any king, or queen, proud. «

DESIGNER
Michael Teipen, CKD, CBD
Kitchens by Teipen
1035 N. State Rd. 135
Greenwood, IN 46142
317-888-7345

SPECIAL FEATURES
Special tile borders; elevated tub; lighted toe kick; back-to-back vanities with mirror.

DIMENSIONS
16' x 16'

PRODUCTS USED
Tile: Limestone on Floor, Tub Deck Pink Slate, Rope Mold Tumbled Marble Border on Backsplashes
Cabinetry: Teipen Custom Cabinetry
Mirrors: Plate Glass on Wall
Sinks: Centura etcetera
Tub, Toilet, Showerhead & Shower Faucets: Koehler
Sink Faucets: Raphael
Vanity Tops: Centura
Lights: Antique Reproduction Hanging in Ceiling

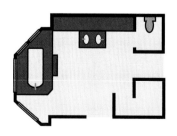

PHOTOGRAPHER: MIKE TEIPEN

Romantic Ambiance

THE UNIQUE CHALLENGE presented to Guita Behbin, of Dura-Maid Industries, was to renovate the master bath in the same home in which this designer remodeled the kitchen, while incorporating the existing extra-deep tub into the new design.

To prevent the tub from being the center of attention, Behbin began by covering the top of the tub with a granite deck and the sides with a short wall of tiles. To increase storage space, a stack of drawers was designed to stand between the two sinks . A shelf along the back of the sink area was also installed, enabling the homeowners to accessorize the bathroom the way they wanted to.

The bathroom, which originally had one lavatory sink on legs and one water closet, now allows husband and wife to luxuriate together with two sinks and a bidet. Light in the room was increased by installing four sconces and a ceiling light controlled by a dimmer switch, creating a level of romantic ambiance.

This classic and soothing design gave the homeowners just what they wanted —a quiet and intimate retreat to revel in, whether together or alone. «

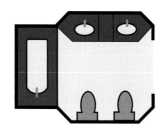

DESIGNER

Guita Behbin
Dura Maid Industries, Inc.
130 Madison Ave.
New York, NY 10016
212-889-6290

SPECIAL FEATURES

Limestone floor tile; glass tile accents; granite tub deck and vanity top; satin nickel fixtures and accessories.

DIMENSIONS

10' x 8'

PRODUCTS USED

Tile: Ann Sacks
Cabinetry: Woodmode
Sinks: American Standard
Tub: Existing
Toilet & Bidet: American Standard
Shower Door: Majestic
Showerhead, Sink Faucets & Shower Faucets: Harrington Brass
Vanity Tops: Granite
Lights: Lee's Lighting

PHOTOGRAPHER: PETER LEDWITH

Pristine and Clean

THIS SOUTHERN CALIFORNIA SPEC HOME had the typical builder decor, including a basic 5-foot tub and surround, minimum-grade sheet vinyl, and a 30-inch-high vanity with two 3-foot-wide drawers. Adding to the original charm, the only source of natural light was a small skylight.

Patricia Knight, of PJ Knight Kitchens, was selected to modernize and customize this bath, which is used primarily by a male teen-ager and overnight guests. Removing the tub and streamlining the materials was Knight's first recommendation. Using one of her favorite artisans, Knight opted for a 13-inch custom mosaic border of palm trees, clouds, waves, and suns. The playful attitude of the spirals in the suns is repeated in the wire and crystal elements of the matte nickel light fixtures and art details on the wall opposite the toilet.

The sealed slate and tile surfaces make this room a snap to clean. What really changed the comfort and cleanup of this bath was AdVent's dual exhaust system, a system which was successful in removing odors inside the bowl, while reducing the spread of germs in the bathroom in general. The Cair-Flow ™ System, installed with the existing ductwork, also removes steam, which can otherwise cause extreme damage to the bath surfaces.

The results of this remodel? A clean and healthy room that's functional and beautiful. «

DESIGNER
Patricia J. Knight
PJ Knight Kitchens, Inc.
814 E. Yanonali St.
Santa Barbara, CA 93103
805-568-3637

SPECIAL FEATURES
Sealed slate and tile surfaces make this room a snap to clean up.

DIMENSIONS
8' x 5'

PRODUCTS USED
Mosaic Tile: available through Tile Showrooms
Ventilation: AdVent International, Inc.
Shower Panel & Door: Majestic Shower Company
Lights: Alfa Lighting, Inc.
Faucet: Ideal Standard
Flooring & Walls: Slate

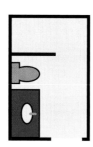

Enlightenment

Desiring a functionally enlarged and brightened luxury bathroom, Robert Weiland, CKD, CBD, of Kitchens by Weiland, transformed his clients' dreams into reality. Utilizing the existing bathroom space plus the small, adjacent walk-in closet, Weiland also borrowed space from a small, connecting bedroom to increase the size of this room. A large, walk-in closet with personalized storage, as well as his and her vanities with storage compartments, now provided these homeowners with a wealth of storage capacity.

To brighten the room, a new arched window was placed behind the 6-foot Whirlpool tub, allowing a view of the garden area and permitting daylight to flood the room. The original ceiling was opened and extended into the attic space creating a cathedral effect, finished with rustic pine boards and beams painted off-white.

The shower enclosure of clear glass allows the tiled walls to flow onto the tub deck, vanity top, and floor creating an exquisite blending of finishes. Bright chrome and brass used on the fixtures, hardware and accessories are the crowning effects, creating a functional and stunning bath facility in which to revel—and unwind. «

DESIGNER
Robert L. Wieland
Kitchens by Wieland, Inc.
4210 Tilghman St.
Allentown, PA 18104-4492
610-395-2074

SPECIAL FEATURES
His and her vanity; oversized glass enclosed showers; cathedral ceiling; makeup area; vanity top with accent tiles.

DIMENSIONS
8' x 19'

PRODUCTS USED
Cabinetry: WilsonArt UltraCraft Laminate
Countertops: Indus Ceramica
Floor Tile and Shower Tile: Indus Ceramica
Sink: Kohler
Water Closet: Kohler Rosario
Whirlpool Tub: Maax-HydroSwirl "Palace"
Plumbing Fixtures: Opella
Shower Door: Easco
Accessories: Cabinet Hardware, Robe Hooks, Towel Shelf-Allied Brass
Chrome Grab Bar-Franklin Brass
Laundry Basket in Cabinet: UltraCraft
Lighting: Juno

Big on Style

THOUGH THIS PREFAB HOME boasts big style, it's quite small on space. The homeowners wanted a bathroom that would adequately provide them both with a place to relax, prep for the day, or unwind in the evening. The challenge was trying to fashion a two-person bathroom and create a separate toilet closet. Sassaman worked with the homeowners to help them solve their dilemma and create a soothing retreat area.

Because the homeowners are often on the beach, they wanted the bathroom to have easy access to and from the coastline. Though the husband originally desired a door providing direct access outside, they scratched that idea in favor of leaving space for a separate tub and shower. To create a glamorous, modern feel, they placed a small chandelier above the Kohler Hat Box toilet. They also installed two showerheads in the shower to satisfy their wish for a two-person room. Cabinetry by Arrital, a resin counter with integrated sink and green glass mosaic tile contribute to the overall ambiance. A telephone next to the toilet and a plasma TV in the toilet room, which can also be viewed from the tub, add to the creature comforts of this soothing retreat.

When faced with the challenge of working big style into a small space, make the most efficient use of what you have by incorporating unique elements into the room. Eye-catching features, such as the chandelier, will draw the eye toward them and away from the size of the space. «

DESIGNER
Howie and Laura Idels

DIMENSIONS
4'6" x 10'

PRODUCTS USED
Tile: Classic Tile
Cabinetry: Arrital
Mirrors: Braun
Sink(s)/counter:
Antonio Miro
Faucet(s): Axor
Tub: Aquatic
Tub Facuet(s):
Antonio Miro
Toilet: Kohler
Showerheads: Grohe
Shower handles: Cifial
Chandelier: James R.
Moder

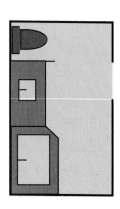

PHOTOGRAPHER: ALISON HAHN

A Suite Match

THE OWNERS of this old Georgian manor built in the early 1900s wanted to remodel their master bath to make it more conducive to their modern lifestyle.

The homeowners were lucky because the original 1900s master suite already had a large space for the master bath, which is rare in older homes. The challenge was to revamp the room into a his-and-her area. To accomplish this, the couple hired Kelly Zamonski, of The Kitchen Place, Inc., in Xenia, Ohio.

To start with, Zamonski gutted the original room down to the framing. Once there, the homeowners faced decisions on how to make their new master suite into a his-and-her area that would best suit their needs.

The original bath had a large old tub that wasn't conducive to the couple's lifestyle. They also needed lots of additional storage areas. The solution: they decided to go with just one walk-in tiled shower. That provided more than enough room for a separate water closet, two linen areas and two vanity areas.

To create a furniture look, Zamonski inserted fluted columns between all the cabinets and on the ends. Each cabinet also had a flush toe with an arched cut-out to create a furniture look. «

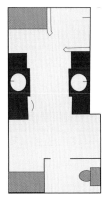

DESIGNER
Kelly Zamonski
The Kitchen Place, Inc.
1163 West Second St.
Xenia, OH 45385
Phone: 937-372-6959

SPECIAL FEATURES
His and her vanities; sit-down makeup area; Fluted column design on vanities & linen closets; built-in linen closets (2); sconces installed against mirrors; flush toe with arched cutouts for furniture look; walk-in shower; staggered depths.

DIMENSIONS
19' x 9'

PRODUCTS USED
Cabinetry: Holiday Kitchens (Elite Construction) Portland Supreme Full **Overlay doorstyle:** Cherry Wood
Flooring: Ceramic Tile
Countertops: Corian
Sink: Integrated Corian
Hardware: Amerock

PHOTOGRAPHER: RAY MCCOY

Window to the World

When Beverly Hills homeowners Ken and Miriam Niver opted to design their master bath, they wanted to create a space that would be large enough to accommodate both of them. They also wished to include ample natural light in the too-dark room.

Due to mitigating factors, a skylight was not possible, and the configuration of the room only allowed for a window on one wall, the wall on which the Nivers wanted to place the tub and shower. To solve the dilemma, the design team, including Mike Federson, created a large, narrow window to span the tub and shower. The window included a dark film to prevent passersby from peeking inside, and a seamless glass shower enclosure separates the shower from the tub. Separate vanities situated on opposite sides provide the couple with their own place to prep.

If attempting to incorporate natural light into a small space such as a bathroom, consider a window, even if the room will only accommodate a narrow design or a skylight. You'll be amazed by how much a little light can transform a dark area. «

DESIGNER
Mike Federson

DIMENSIONS
15' x 10'

PRODUCTS USED
Tile/stone: Limestone
Cabinetry: Custom
Countertops: Limestone
Mirror: Custom with limestone frame
Sink(s): Kohler
Tub: Kohler
Shower doors: Custom by Paul & Assoc.
Toilet: Kohler

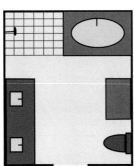

Zen Sophistication

SERENE WAS THE KEY DESCRIPTIVE WORD the homeowners used when describing their ideal for their new master bath. As in many baths, space was a premium, and all involved worked to reconfigure the room's layout to optimize storage and maintain a minimalist result rich in details and materials but not overwhelming.

To create a room that looked deceivingly large, the contractor brought the floor tile up onto the countertops and walls, which gave the illusion of more expansive surfaces and made the space appear much bigger.

The designer used clean designs with an emphasis on materials, not decoration. Dark-wood cabinetry provided a visual punch, but was not overdone and did not overpower the space. The design was so simple it has a Zen-like quality, and in keeping with the principles of Zen, the room was created for maximum bliss. The artwork in the room had an Asian flavor, and even the frosted glass reminded visitors of an Oriental folding screen.

The universal style used for the sinks allowed for the unique counter tile installation with reduced-depth storage below. The towel ledge and vanity cubbies allowed for the display of luxurious bath accessories and gave the room added interest and depth.

Serene was what the homeowners wanted, but they also got a simple, sophisticated, and stunning master bath that will never go out of style. «

DESIGNER
Karen Bieszczak, CKD
Bzak Design Group
614 Wooster Pike
Terrace Park, OH 45174
513-831-3155

SPECIAL FEATURES
Modern, rich wood tones; pebble accents; universal design sink basins

DIMENSIONS
10' x 14'

PRODUCTS USED
Tile: Casa Fascia Giottoli pebbles; 8x8 Botticino
Cabinetry: Holiday Seattle cherry with onyx glaze
Mirrors: Ryan's All Glass
Sink(s): Vitra
Tub: Kohler Mariposa
Toilet: Kohler
Shower Door: Ryan's All Glass
Showerhead: Grohe
Sink Faucets: Kohler Memoirs
Shower Facuets: Grohe
Vanity Top: 8x8 Botticino
Lights: Central Light
Plumbing Supplies: Keidel Supply
Drawer Pulls: Amerock

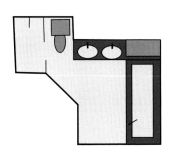

PHOTOGRAPHER: DAVID STEINBRUNNER

Below-Grade Beauty

THINGS AREN'T ALWAYS what they seem. In this case, what appears to be a spacious, yet straightforward, master bath was actually carved out of a laundry room, utility room, and half bath.

The homeowners of the split-level home asked for a master bath off a lower level bedroom, and after 18 years in the kitchen and bath remodeling business, Jim Gerson, of Custom Crafters, Inc., in Kensington, Maryland, was up to the project. The homeowners knew Gerson's work because they had previously contracted him for their kitchen remodel with great success. "There is just no substitution for experience when creating a new room from raw space," Gerson explains.

He gutted the collection of small spaces, then combined and reorganized, keeping laundry facilities close at hand. Heating and air ducts had to be extensively rerouted to maintain a generous ceiling height, and a window was replaced. Materials were carefully considered to accommodate the slab foundation. From the rubble, Gerson created room for a 6-foot soaking tub, a 42-by-42-inch shower and plenty of storage in a tall linen cabinet.

Bright colors, ample lighting, delicate floral wallpaper, and large floor tiles give the room a light, airy feel, even though it is mostly below grade. The result is a bath that completes the lower level suite and serves as a restful space to start or end the day. «

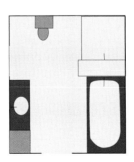

DESIGNER
Jim Gerson
Custom Crafters Inc.
4000 Howard Ave.
Kensington, MD 20895
301-493-4000

SPECIAL FEATURES
Soaking tub, generous shower, linen storage

DIMENSIONS
10'10" x 9'6"

PRODUCTS USED
Tile: Florida Tile, floral pastel
Cabinetry: Schrock, Gentry oak
Mirrors: Schrock, Gentry oak
Sink(s): Waldorf cultured marble
Tub: Kohler Portrait
Toilet: Kohler Portrait
Shower Door: Alumax
Showerhead: Moen
Sink Faucets: Moen, Traditional Cross
Shower Faucets: Moen, Monticello
Vanity Tops: Waldorf cultured marble
Lights: Nutone
Exhaust Fan: Nutone
Plumbing Supplies: Kohler
Drawer Pulls: C.H. Briggs Hardware

PHOTOGRAPHER: MICHAEL VENTURA

Suite and Light

DESIGNING A NEW HOME is fun but not always easy. Reconciling wants, needs, and dreams with budgets and construction realities can be a challenge. And sometimes it is difficult to visualize what a room is actually going to look and feel like. This obstacle was overcome when the homeowners and Chris Dreith, of The Home Improvements Group, met to lay out their master bathroom.

Concerned that some of the elements of their conceptual drawings might reduce the amount of desired natural light, the couple and the designer took tape to the floor of the couple's barn, carefully outlining the floor plan and getting a feel for the space. They then took bee boxes—the owners are beekeepers—and constructed walls and vanities, creating a very real idea of what was to come.

In the actual construction of the room, Dreith placed angled, mirrored closet doors on either side of the dramatic entry, which allows an open, bright space centered on the unique vanity. A tower that houses open shelves, small accessory drawers, and a tamboured appliance garage separate his and her sinks. A small peninsula increases storage and counter space without blocking light from the glass block walls of the shower. The toilet room includes additional tall storage cabinets.

A little ingenuity in the planning stage resulted in a luxurious, light-filled master suite that the homeowners love. «

DESIGNER
Chris Dreith, CKD, CBD
The Home
Improvements Group Inc.
440 Main St.
Woodland, CA 95695
530-666-5061

SPECIAL FEATURES
Glass block walls in large walk-in shower; unique vanity with center peninsula; window above vanity mirrors

DIMENSIONS
15' x 15'

PRODUCTS USED:
Cabinetry: Merit
Vanity Tops: WilsonArt Gibralter solid surfacing
Drawer Pulls: Notting Hill Decorative Hardware

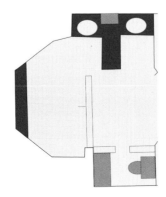

PHOTOGRAPHER: STEVE WHITSITT

Lavish Luxury

As part of the second-story addition to her own Beverlycrest estate, Nicole Sassaman fashioned this master bathroom to function as a personal escape from her professional pace. She also wanted to incorporate a variety of well-designed elements into the room.

In an effort to create understated elegance, Sasssaman chose the Kohler Purist Infinity bathtub to serve as the focal point. Modeled after an infinity pool, the tub is designed to harness the simple beauty of water as it flows over all four sides into a catch pool below. Sassaman also crafted a curved vanity and placed two Lefroy Brooks sink vessels atop it. She laid Lagos Azul slabs and a creamy limestone mosaic for the floors, both from Walker Zanger.

When designing the steam shower, Sassaman was challenged with the task of including benches without overcrowding the space. To solve the dilemma, she opted for two teak fold-up benches by Waterworks. The result is a rich contrast to the light-hued stone and other dark elements. When faced with the problem of attempting to crowd a desired feature into limited space, research other options. You may be surprised to find how well plan B coordinates with your space. «

DESIGNER
Nicole Sassaman Designs

DIMENSIONS
18' x 10'

PRODUCTS USED
Cabinetry: Custom
Mirrors: Custom
Sink(s): Lefroy Brooks
Faucet(s): Newport Brass
Tub: Kohler
Toilet: Kohler Memoirs
Shower bench:
Waterworks
Floors: Walker Zanger
Hardware: Details

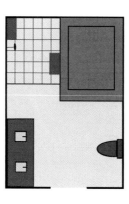

PHOTOGRAPHER: ALISON HAHN

Marvelous in Malibu

THE BATHROOM in this Malibu, California, home needed a remodel. The existing configuration featured a crooked, poorly framed wall adorned with too many plugs and switches. To help revive the ailing space, Nicole Sassaman suggested covering the wall with stone. This solution created a beautiful design element and prevented the homeowners from having to reframe and drywall.

More than merely an intriguing finished product, even the process of placing the stones was enjoyable. "It made it feel like you were in a cave-like bathroom or even an ancient castle," Sassaman said. To balance this old-world aesthetic, Sassaman selected modern fixtures. She also installed a double showerhead and mosaic tile that overflows into the shower.

If ever faced with a design dilemma involving an unsightly wall, consider refacing the exterior with a creative material such as stone. In this case, the rich texture and varying depths of the stone masked the unattractive, crooked wall beneath. «

DESIGNER
Nicole Sassaman Designs

DIMENSIONS
5' x 9'

PRODUCTS USED
Stone: Walker Zanger
Cabinetry: Waterworks
Mirror(s): West Elm
Sink(s): Waterworks
Faucet(s): Newport Brass
Tub: Kathryn by Kohler
Toilet: Kohler
Floors: Mosaic limestone

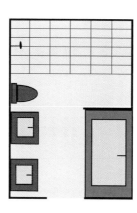

PHOTOGRAPHER: ALISON HAHN

Inventive on the Avenue

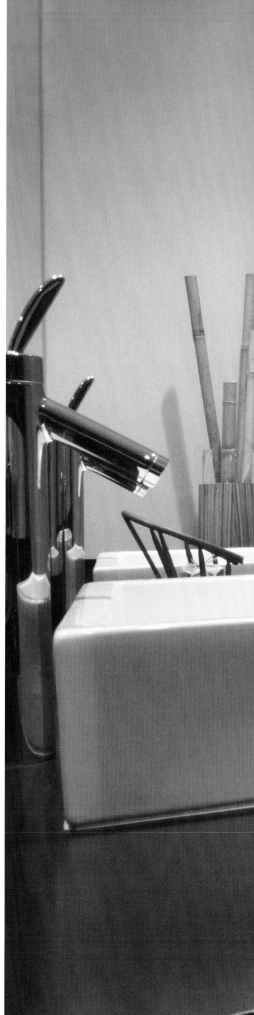

THOUGH THE AVENUE OF THE STARS is a desirable address, the master bath in this Los Angeles high rise was not so. A wall separating the dressing room from the bathroom rendered the spaces too small, and it was inconvenient to have to pass through both rooms. To remedy the issue, Nicole Sassaman removed the wall, which necessitated the removal of the back shower wall. To maintain a sense of openness, she replaced the shower wall with glass.

To retain a wall long enough to accommodate two sinks, Sassaman had to keep an existing hallway. This layout, however, forced residents to make a near U-turn to enter the bathroom. In an effort to ensure that the tricky entrance not trump the design, Sassaman installed a mirrored backsplash between upper and lower cabinets. This mirror allows residents to view the reflection of the bath immediately upon entrance.

Within the shower, Sassaman installed a teak fold-up bench. A large limestone slab composes the walls and creates a beautiful, seamless aesthetic. Finally, she installed a fixed pane of glass for the shower door that stretched to the ceiling. By having the glass meet the ceiling, she was able to affix the swinging door to the fixed pane. «

DESIGNER
Nicole Sassaman Designs

DIMENSIONS
9'6" x 6'6"

PRODUCTS USED
Stone: Walker Zanger
Cabinetry: Custom
Sink(s): Lefroy Brooks
Faucet(s): Philippe Starck
Toilet: Kohler
Shower fixtures: Kohler
Floors: Custom walnut

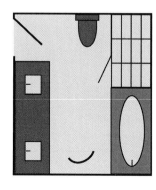

PHOTOGRAPHER: ALISON HAHN

World Travelers

HAVING TRAVELED AND LIVED in numerous countries during their lives, these clients knew what a true luxury bathroom experience could be. As guests in some of the world's finest hotels, they wished to bring some of the luxury they had experienced into their own master bath.

To achieve this comfort and sophistication, they called upon Steven Joel Meltzer, of Abbey's Kitchens, Baths and Interiors, Inc. Collaborating, they elected to demolish the existing master bedroom and adjacent bathroom, then to reconfigure the space, making the bedroom smaller and increasing the bath-suite area. To compensate for downsizing the bedroom, the new room boasts a vaulted ceiling, which creates the illusion of a much larger space.

The luxury list of amenities for the dream bath included a multi-jet whirlpool tub, heated floor system built under the tiles, combination steam room/shower area, tall storage areas for linens and personal-care items, custom-opaqued frameless glass partitions for the toilet and shower room, makeup desk area with illuminated magnifying pull-out mirror, and a walk-in closet adjacent to the room.

Now, no matter where this family may travel, they can be sure that their own bath retreat would be the envy of any sophisticated world traveler. «

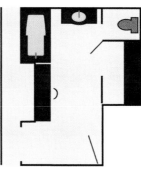

DESIGNER
Steven Joel Meltzer
Abbey's Kitchens, Baths
and Interiors Inc.
38 Chatham Road Suite 4
Short Hills, NJ 07078
923-376-8878

SPECIAL FEATURES
Custom steam room;
heated floor; custom
shower enclosure

DIMENSIONS
19' x 15'

PRODUCTS USED
Tile: Standard Tile Corp.
Cabinetry: Superior
Woodcraft
Vanity Tops: Orchetto
Marble: Bedrock Granite
Sinks: Kohler
Sink Faucets: California
Faucets
Mirrors: Ton Jon
Toilet: Toto
Lighting: Custom
Fixtures
Drawer Pulls: Cliffside
Industries
Tub: MTI Whirlpool
Shower Faucets: Ondine
Adlon
Shower Door: Century
Glasstec Shower Door
Showerhead: Ondine
Adlon
Accessories: Samuel
Heath

ACCESSORIES: SAMUEL HEATH

Modern Elegance

When the homeowners decided to add a master bath and closet area, they called upon designer R. Thom Brawner, of Miller's Fancy Bath & Kitchen. They wanted a luxurious and relaxing space and gave Brawner free reign to create it for them. The focal point is the large Palladian window. A barrel-vaulted ceiling runs the entire length of the bath, with an iron and alabaster chandelier above the oversized whirlpool.

His and her vanities have neoclassic furniture detailing, granite countertops, and undermount china bowls. Each has a triple-door mirrored cabinet with interior electric outlets and vertical side lighting. Heated travertine marble floors enhance the large room. The whirlpool decking is made of the same marble, giving the room a sense of fluidity and continuity. A separate walk-in shower room features dual showerheads and multiple body sprays. The shower walls and ceiling repeat the use of travertine in combination with glass block in a stepped design. This affords privacy without sacrificing light.

Massive stone columns flank the open entrance of the master bedroom and are repeated in the middle of the bath as a frame for the whirlpool decking. The bath features a breakfast bar and a walk-in closet with custom-designed built-in cabinetry. Adding to the modern elegance, French doors lead to an adjoining garden that overlooks a private lake. «

DESIGNER
R. Thom Brawner
Miller's Fancy Bath &
Kitchen
3730 Lexington Road
Louisville, KY 40207
502-893-9330

SPECIAL FEATURES
Barrel vaulted ceiling;
custom furniture-look
vanity cabinetry; his
and her triple medicine
cabinets with vertical
lights and interior
electric

DIMENSIONS
17' x 29'

PRODUCTS USED
Tile: Travertine Marble
Cabinetry: Custom
Cabinet
Mirrors: Robern
Sink(s): Kohler Caxton
China Undermount
Tub: Jason Madeline
Toilet: Kolher Memoirs
Classic
Showerhead: Altmans
Sink Faucets: Altmans
Shower Faucets:
Altmans
Vanity Tops: Gallio
Veneziana
Lighting: Robern
Vertical Incandescent
Drawer Pulls: Anne At
Home

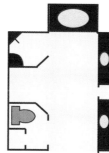

PHOTOGRAPHER: KENNETH HAGAN

Colonial Master Bath

WHEN THE CLIENTS DECIDED to build their dream home in northwest suburban Chicago, they contacted Nick G. Virgilio, CGR, of Janco Design Group, Inc. They asked him not only to assist in the design process, but ultimately to build their lavish golf-course home with a beautiful walk-out view of the No. 2 tee and fairway. Virgilio used his kitchen and bath design experience to assist in the design of the kitchen and four baths. The master bath was of special interest to the couple, because it was to be their own personal space.

Because the bath is located on interior walls between the bedroom and walk-in closet, natural light was a prime concern. This challenge was met by installing a skylight in the vaulted ceiling above the tub. The natural light is enhanced by the large expanse of wall mirror above the tub and vanities, visually adding to the room's already ample dimensions.

The tub, which is the focal point, has a stone-look ceramic tile deck and splash area coupled with custom cherry woodworking on the apron. The cherry matches the flanking wall-hung vanities, which are finished off with granite tops as well as chrome and brass fixtures. To add privacy to the toilet area while maintaining the open feeling, a stepped glass-block divider was installed. The bath truly feels like an integral part of the master suite. «

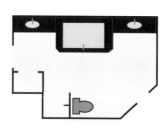

DESIGNER
Nick G. Virgilio
Janco Design Group, Inc.
236 Crest Ct.
Bloomingdale, IL 60108
630-529-2487

SPECIAL FEATURES
Skylight; vaulted ceiling; matching cherry tub apron

DIMENSIONS
12' x 18'

PRODUCTS USED
Tile: Florida Tile
Cabinetry: Merit-Cherry
Sink(s): Kohler
Tub: MTI
Toilet: Kohler
Shower Door: Alumax
Showerhead: Grohe
Drawer Pulls: Bamal Corporation
Sink Faucets: Moen
Shower Faucets: Grohe
Vanity tops: Granite
Advent Toilet Vent
System, MTI Shower
Base

PHOTOGRAPHER: SUE RICHERT

Old World Elegance

IN KEEPING WITH THE AMBIANCE of this new multi-million-dollar lake home, Carol Lindell, owner of DCI Kitchen and Bath, created a master bath that combines the look of traditional furniture with the most modern features and functions. The home was featured in the 2000 Homerama in Charlotte, North Carolina. DCI Kitchen and Bath provided cabinetry and built-ins throughout the award-winning home, including the main kitchen, lake-level wet bar/kitchen, master suite, laundry room, and multiple bathrooms.

The master bath was fully integrated to complement the overall design of the master suite. Cabinetry is detailed to include convex reeded pilasters and dentil crown, which were also featured on the bedroom's four-poster bed and custom-designed armoire/wet bar (also provided by DCI). Within the abundant space of this bath, Carol's design focused on providing day-to-day storage for bath linens, toiletries, and bathroom appliances, while creating the feeling of an elegant, Old World landowner's retreat. «

DESIGNER
Carol Lindell
Design Centers
International / DCI
Kitchen and Bath
1300 South Blvd, Suite C
Charlotte, NC 28203
704-926-6000

SPECIAL FEATURES
Countertop vanity cabinetry with mullion doors and small drawers flank his vanity. The arched valance reflects design details from the master bath whirlpool enclosure, with dentil crown and convex reeded pilasters echoing the master bedroom's cabinetry and 4-poster bed. Her area includes a custom-detailed corner vanity seating area with lighting concealed by its arched valance. Left of the corner unit is the chest-on-chest amoire furniture / storage unit, with her sink area to the right including ample shelving on either side of the mirror.

DIMENSIONS
22' x 14'

PRODUCTS USED
Cabinetry: Quality Custom, Provence Raised Panel Door in Olde Town Yellow
Tile & Countertops: Natural Stone

PHOTOGRAPHER: SOUTHERN EXPOSURE

A Stroke Of Genius

THE OWNERS of this classic brick ranch home dreamed of an elegant bath but needed help coping with the existing limitations. Their modest bathroom, an outdated and unimaginative space, opened directly into the family dining room and detracted from the visual appeal.

George Kennedy, of Kennedy Kitchens & Baths, was able to see past these challenges and create an outstanding solution. The homeowners were delighted when Kennedy showed them how relocating the bathroom entry door to an adjacent hallway would make better use of the space, produce an exciting new layout, and even "enlarge" the dining room by reclaiming the wall where the door had been.

After gutting the bathroom and cutting the new doorway, Kennedy installed rich-cherry custom cabinetry in the corner of the room that is now visible from the hallway. The two countertop levels of the sink vanity and the dressing table create visual interest and make each space more functional. Crowning touches include matching cherry soffits, mirror moldings, and beautiful curio display shelves tucked neatly into the corner. Halogen lighting and large mirrors make a bright and inviting space. «

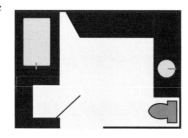

DESIGNER
George Kennedy
Kennedy Kitchens and
Baths
1212 North Street
Springfield, IL 62704
217-793-2284

SPECIAL FEATURES
Cherry custom cabinets; multi-level countertops; matching cherry mouldings and soffits; cultured marble tub walls, floor tiles, base board trim.

DIMENSIONS
8' x 8'

PRODUCTS USED
Tile: Cultured Marble "Antique White"
Cabinetry: Prestige "Cherry"
Vanity Tops: Cultured Marble "Antique White"
Sink(s): Cultured Marble "Antique White"
Tub: Ultra Bath
Sink Faucets: Concinnity
Toilet: Kohler
Shower Door: Workright ¼ inch Glass
Showerhead: Moen
Shower faucets: Moen
Drawer Pulls: Concinnity "Polished Brass"

Attention To Details

BRIGHT AND BEAUTIFUL, this elegant master bath is the perfect place to escape. The space, designed by George Kennedy of Kennedy Kitchen Distributors, is part of a new home. Among its many luxurious features is a Pearl whirlpool tub surrounded by large windows that overlook a panorama of timber and rolling farmland. Matching his and her adult-height cherry vanities were manufactured by Prestige in a rich paprika tone. The front of the whirlpool is trimmed with the cabinet doors matching the full-overlay cherry in the vanities. In addition to coordinating beautifully with the other woods, these FFD frame doors also provide convenient access to the whirlpool motor. Adjacent to the main vanity/tub area is a private space containing a 5-foot-wide shower and water closet.

Kennedy emphasized that the key to a successful design project is to go to the site during construction and measure everything, rather than to trust drawings, which may not be wholly accurate. "There was no room for error on this master bath, as the tub and custom vanities had to fit exactly," he said. "That's why our slogan is 'We measure up.' " «

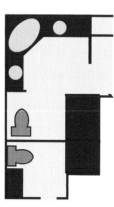

DESIGNER
George Kennedy
Kennedy Kitchens &
Baths
1212 North Street
Springfield, IL 62704
217-793-2284

SPECIAL FEATURES
Cherry custom cabinets; matching his and her vanities; matching cherry mouldings; cultured marble tub backsplash; base board trim.

DIMENSIONS
10' x 10'

PRODUCTS USED
Tile: Cultured Marble "White-White"
Cabinetry: Prestige "Cherry"
Vanity Tops: Cultured Marble "White-White"
Sink(s): Cultured Marble "White-white"
Tub: Pearl
Sink Faucets: Moen
Toilet: Kohler
Shower Door: Workright ¼-inch Glass
Showerhead: Moen
Shower faucets: Moen
Drawer Pulls: Signature Hardware

PHOTOGRAPHER: STEVE HINRICHS

Elegant Reflections

INVITING, COMFORTABLE, AND ELEGANT were the traits that this fun couple had in mind when planning their new master suite.

The major challenge of creating this bath was working with a large room with a domed ceiling. "It was important to make this spacious room feel warm and inviting for my clients," says Sandra Soine, designer at Kitchen Gallery of Spring Grove.

Soine accomplished her goal by framing the mirrors with matching maple wood and crown molding to help soften the ceiling height. Placing a tall wall cabinet in the center of the two vanities enhanced the long run of cabinets and mirrors. Mirrored doors on the wall cabinet, along with sconces on the sides, brightly illuminated the space.

Surrounded with glass block and a large window overlooking a beautiful wooded backyard, the whirlpool and deck are large enough to accommodate two people for a romantic bath or just one who wants to enjoy a long, relaxing soak in the tub. As if that weren't enough appeal, Soine created storage space under the whirlpool. With the help of Jay Soine and his team from Granite Edge, the deck and vanity were topped with granite to complete the flow of warmth and contrasting color.

All combined, Soine designed a space where her clients feel like kicking off their shoes, grabbing a towel, and making this bath a relaxing retreat. «

DESIGNER
Sandra R. Soine
Kitchen Gallery of Spring Grove
2404 Suite C Spring Ridge Dr.
Spring Grove, IL 60081
815-675-6900

SPECIAL FEATURES
Matching maple cabinets and mirror frames; glass blocks around shower door

DIMENSIONS
16' x 19'

PRODUCTS USED
Cabinetry: Dura Supreme
Sink(s): Toto
Shower Door: Glass Blocks
Toilet: Kohler
Sink Faucet: KWC
Vanity Tops: Uba Tuba granite

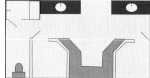

PHOTOGRAPHER: STEVE WHITSITT

Natural Masterpiece

WITH A DESIRE FOR ELEGANCE and spacious relaxation in their bathroom, homeowners in a Chicago suburb called upon designer Rick J. Ruzanski, CKBR, of Distinctive Home Improvements, to meet their remodeling needs. A more luxurious shower and cabinetry dresser space were on the list of creations that brought transformation to the preexisting builder-grade features of the bathroom to a custom level. It didn't take long to discover that the soaker tub had to go and gutting was required in order to create more space; doing a room addition simply wasn't cost effective.

Ruzanski faced several interesting challenges. First was the issue of creating as much cabinet space as possible in the alcove, which previously housed the bathtub. Creating a U-shape area of built-in tall dresser cabinets with custom open shelves flanking the three-sided cabinet layout solved this problem. Installing a shower seat helped gain additional space in the shower.

Pulling the dresser cabinetry together with the existing angles called for creativity in designing open shelves. The new bathroom plan provides for an interesting layout without changing the locations of the two walk-in bathroom closets or other key components. Natural slate tiles, sleek granite countertops, and rich burgundy cabinetry enhance the natural feel of the bathroom. «

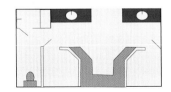

DESIGNER
Rick Ruzanski
Detailed Builders, Inc.
417 Quentin Rd
Palatine, IL 60067
847-991-9586

SPECIAL FEATURES
Built-in dresser cabinets replaced whirlpool tub; custom shower

DIMENSIONS
20' x 10'

PRODUCTS USED
Tile: Slate with grout
Cabinetry: B.C.S. frameless raised panel
Mirrors: Custom
Sink(s): Kohler
Toilet: Kohler
Shower Door: Custom frameless
Showerhead: Kohler Georges IV
Sink Faucets: Kohler Georges IV
Shower Faucets: Kohler Georges IV
Vanity Tops: Tropical brown granite
Lights: Task
Ceiling Fans: Casablanca
Drawer Pulls: Satin nickel oval
Door hardware: Schlage Accent

PHOTOGRAPHER: STEVE WHITSITT

Fab Features

WHEN THE OWNER of this home decided to remodel the bathroom, Rick J. Ruzanski, CKBR, of Distinctive Home Improvements, was asked to do more than just change a few fixtures and change the wall covering. He completely gutted the space and created an entirely new design. The challenge, however, was fitting into the same space an extensive wish list. From an oversized whirlpool bath to an entertainment center, the homeowner had visions of grandeur for the space.

In order to accommodate the new whirlpool bath with river rapids, along with a larger custom shower and bidet, the existing bathroom space was merged with a large walk-in closet within the bathroom. Using the existing walk-in closet added approximately 30 square feet of living space to allow for a large custom shower, additional new location for the commode, and enough space to add a bidet.

The space for the existing linen storage cabinet was converted into a combination entertainment center and linen storage cabinet. The upper portion provided the perfect space to hide audio equipment and a television, while the lower portion could be utilized for linen storage.

While planning every new element of the bathroom, the designer had to work around an existing window niche in order to avoid making any renovations to the home's exterior.

The result is a customized space with features found in few other bathrooms. «

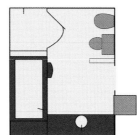

DESIGNER
Rick Ruzanski
Detailed Builders, Inc.
417 Quentin Rd
Palatine, IL 60067
847-991-9586

SPECIAL FEATURES
Large custom shower; therapeutic type whirlpool tub; entertainment center type cabinet; bidet; in-floor radiant heat; towel warmer; glass vessel sink.

DIMENSIONS
12' 1" x 11' 1"

PRODUCTS USED
Cabinetry: Jay Rambo
Tile: Palisandra Classico
Mirrors: Robern
Sink(s): Kohler
Tub: Kohler Riverbath
Toilet: Kohler
Shower Door: Custom
Sink Faucets: Kohler Cirrus
Shower Faucets: Kohler Showertower
Vanity Tops: 2cm Palisandra Classico
Lights: Robern/ Casablanca
Drawer P: Dekkor
Bidet: Kohler
Towel Bars and Accessories: Kohler
Towel Warmer: Walney
In Floor Heat: Warmly Yours

PHOTOGRAPHER: STEVEN PAUL WHITSITT

Find More Space

A BATHROOM only 5 feet wide was just too small for the owners of this Long Island home. They called on designer Fara Boico to help them "find more space." They asked Boico to create a new bathroom that the couple could share comfortably. They wanted more elbow room, including separate his and her vanities. Other requests included an extra-large shower and a whirlpool tub.

Boico increased the overall space by borrowing from an adjacent walk-in closet. The tub deck was extended into the shower area to serve as a shower seat and topped with Corian to match the counters. On the far side, a knee wall was placed to provide privacy around the water closet.

Custom cabinetry finished in a coffee stain was used for the vanities, both with ample storage and counter space. Hers includes a seating area—perfect for applying makeup or hair styling. Custom boutique boxes are recessed into the walls over both vanities for additional storage. Boico supplemented the illumination with several high-hat recessed fixtures. Ceramic wall tile is highlighted by a decorative chair-rail border, repeated in the tub deck. Soffits were lowered to frame out the shapes of the vanities, shower stall and whirlpool. Boico finished the soffits in ceramic tile and used crown molding for design interest at the ceiling. The natural limestone look on the floor was achieved with maintenance-free ceramic tiles, making cleanup a breeze. «

DESIGNER
Fara Boico
Classic Kitchen & Bath Center, Ltd.
1062 Northern Blvd.,
Roslyn, NY 11576
516-621-7700

60 B Jobs Lane,
Southampton, NY 11968
631-204-9500

SPECIAL FEATURES
His and her vanities with lots of storage and counter space; custom angled shower with seat and pressure-balanced shower valve for safety; easy to maintain surfaces; decorative tile border on walls and tub deck; recessed custom boutique boxes above vanities

DIMENSIONS
13'6" x 8'6"

PRODUCTS USED
Cabinetry: Private Label
Flooring: Sichenia ceramic tile
Counters: DuPont Corian
Sink(s): Corian Integral Bowl
Faucets: Watermark
Whirlpool tub: Jacuzzi
Fixtures: Kohler
Shower: Custom
Wallcovering: Ceramic tile; Custom boutique boxes

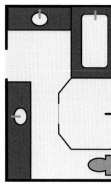

PHOTOGRAPHER: BILL BUSCH

Winning Perfection

THIS AWE-INSPIRING BATH WON A **NKBA** AWARD for Best Master Suite/Bathroom for Jim Meloy, CKD and his design team at Kitchen and Bath Concepts. Expansion and integration in this 30-year-old home were the key elements for the completion of the dream-like suite. By sacrificing a spare bedroom to gain space and removing walls, the master bath, closet and bedroom could be fused as one room. Incorporated into the space was the clients' long list of requests, including a dressing area, ample storage space, separate vanities with vessel sinks, plenty of closet space, a corner tub, shower with rainhead and separate water closet with bidet.

Meloy blended the design with various textured materials to please the homeowners. The floor, walls, vertical cabinet bases, tub and shower are tiled in copper slate with inserts of mosaic basket weave tile. Slate rails and bars act as frames for the vanity mirrors. The vessel bowls, tub, toilet, bidet, ceiling and shutters are painted white to offset the black cabinets and copper slate. The shower was constructed of clear glass halfway to the ceiling on three sides to create several viewpoints of the spacious room. Selecting unique materials, an incredible lighting program, and design details transformed this space into a winning master bath for both clients and design team. «

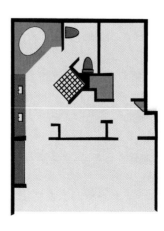

DESIGNER
Jim Meloy, CKD
Kitchen and Bath
Concepts
11444 Alpharetta Hwy.
Roswell, GA 30076
770-442-9845
770-664-3674

SPECIAL FEATURES
Basket weave tile;
tile-framed mirrors;
open storage in vanity
cabinets

DIMENSIONS
19' x 16'

PRODUCTS USED
Tile: Indian Copper Slate
with mosaic basket
weave tile inserts
Cabinetry: Corsi
Cabinets
Sink: Le Bijou
Tub: Kohler
Toilet: Kohler
Showerhead: Grohe
Sink Faucets: Kohler
Shower Faucets: Grohe
Vanity tops: Atlantic
Green granite
Drawer pulls: Top Knobs

PHOTOGRAPHER: JIM MELOY

Design of the Vanity

THIS SMALL BATHROOM RECEIVED AN EXTREME MAKEOVER when it was fully gutted and remodeled. Because the homeowners have a relatively small family and do not open their home to entertaining often, there were no requirements to create the bathroom in such a way that it would be conducive to the traffic of numerous guests. The homeowner's main objective was to enhance the aesthetic value of the room and to create the vanity as the focal point of the bathroom.

Jack Slubowski, of Homewood Kitchen & Bath, Inc., was employed to bring the homeowner's dream bathroom to completion. Intending to successfully create an eye-catching vanity that would serve as the room's centerpiece was a challenge. Slubowski and the homeowners approached this challenge head on and decided upon the implementation of custom cabinetry with custom legs and supports for a sandblasted glass top. These elements combined to result in an appealing vanity.

The addition of a lighted wall for the careful spotlighting of pictures to the left of the vanity further enhances the room's ambience. A location was recessed into the wall, and low voltage lighting was used to light the space. The finished project is a bathroom that glows with subtle warmth and highlights the beauty of the unique vanity. «

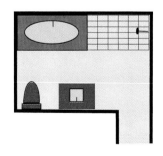

DESIGNER
Jack Slubowski
Homewood Kitchen &
Bath, Inc.
18027 Dixie Highway
Homewood, IL 60430
708-799-0176

SPECIAL FEATURES
Custom cabinetry;
custom legs and
supports; sandblasted
glass top

DIMENSIONS
9' x 8'

PRODUCTS USED
Tile: Ceramic and
glass tiles
Cabinetry
The Hampshire Co.
Mirrors: Advance Glass
& Paint Co.
Sink(s): Deco Lav
Whirlpool: MTI
Toilet: Kohler
Shower Door: Advance
Glass & Paint Co.
Showerhead: Grohe
Sink Faucets: Kohler
Shower Faucets: Grohe
Vanity Top: Advance
Glass & Paint Co.
Lights: Task Lighting Corp.
Shower Base:
Swanstone
Vanity legs and
countertop supports:
Eskay Metal Fabricating

Midwest Makeover

DESIGNER
James C. Moore
Jan Merrell Kitchens
901 Jefferson Avenue
Toledo, OH 43624
419-246-0991
419-246-0950

SPECIAL FEATURES
Custom shower and
vanity; heated floor;
towel warmer; custom
tile work

DIMENSIONS
12' x 18'

PRODUCTS USED
Flooring: Florentine
limestone tiles
Cabinetry: Downsview
"Moda" door style in
Java Satinwood
Sink: Kohler Caxton
undermount
Tub: Kohler Iron Works
Whirlpool
Shower Door: Custom
Vanity Top: Zodiac
Quartz in Astral Pearl
Shower Plumbing:
Kohler 2-Way body
spray, hand shower;
Altman Shower
Rose; Grohe control,
thermostat control
Vanity: Grohe Talia
Tub: Grohe Talia tub
spout
Towel Warmer: Myson
Electric Towel Warmer
Mirrors: Custom

THE OWNERS OF THIS HOME both manage hectic
schedules, but they wanted to ensure their few
moments together in the bath would be relaxing
and intimate. Their dream was to have a calming
environment that incorporated lavish details. After the
couple met with bathroom designer James C. Moore,
they realized their renovation would quickly turn into
a renovation/expansion.

Moore incorporated elegant java satinwood in a
Downsview "moda" door style for an updated twist on the
cabinetry. The limestone-faced, curved, walk-in shower
built for two features a bench and chrome body sprays.
A rain-style showerhead massager completes the serene
ambiance throughout the bathroom.

Because Midwestern winters can make exiting the
shower unpleasant, Moore installed a towel warmer and
a luxurious heated floor to keep the
couple's toes toasty warm. The new
custom-designed zodiac quartz vanity
allows each homeowner the luxury of
having their own well-lit area. Glass
mosaic tiles accompanied by custom-cut
limestone window casements add modern decadence. The homeowners' love for
artistic detail is evident throughout this
new classically designed wing. «

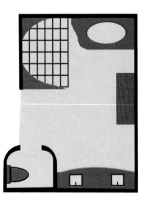

PHOTOGRAPHER: STEVEN PAUL WHITSITT

A Suite Retreat

THE OWNERS of this Princeton Junction, New Jersey, home wanted to change the style of their bathroom to accommodate something more in-line with their discerning tastes. They gave designer John Lang, of Lang's Traditions Kitchen and Bath, and Fran Pappas a simple edict: keep everything white in color, but stay in tune with the look and design of the rest of the house.

The toughest challenge, Lang said, was removing an old fireplace from the room. Doing this cleared the way to relocate the massive 6-foot tub and created space for a custom shower, complete with tiled columns of Alabastro porcelain and tumbled limestone. The extra space also accommodated an area for a beautiful granite vanity.

The original bathroom had two entrances. Removing one led to a custom closet renovation that allows accessibility from the bathroom without disturbing anyone who might be sleeping in the bedroom. In keeping with the family's desire to "keep everything white in color," Jay Rambo cabinetry was finished in a glaze that provided a country French look.

Once the home of an outdated fireplace, this room now offers the inviting warmth sure to spark a search for more reasons to spend time in this retreat. «

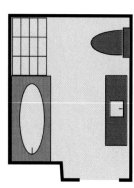

DESIGNER
John A. Lang
Lang's Traditions
Kitchen and Bath
9 Summit Square Center
RT. 413 & RT. 332
Langhorne, PA 19047
215-860-4143
215-860-3920

SPECIAL FEATURES
Whirlpool tub; custom glass shower door; cabinets to countertops for extra space; multi shower body sprays

DIMENSIONS
15' x 12'

PRODUCTS USED
Tile: Alabastro porcelain, tumbled limestone
Cabinetry: Jay Rambo
Mirrors: Custom glass
Sinks: Kohler
Tub: Kohler
Toilet: Kohler
Shower Door: Easco
Vanity Tops: Granite
Plumbing Supplies: Ondine, Jaclo

DESIGNER
Rebecca Gullion
Lindquist
Lindquist and Company
926 East 4th St.
Duluth, MN 55805
218-728-5171

SPECIAL FEATURES
Undermount whirlpool
tub; Corian shower with
bench seat; glass block
wall; custom stainless-
steel safety grab bars;
stainless-steel valances;
in-floor heat; wall-
mounted toilet and bidet

DIMENSIONS
10' x 10'

PRODUCTS USED
Floor tile: Latco
Wainscot tile: ceramic
Cabinetry: Wood-Mode
Series 84 in Natural
Cherry
Sink(s): Dupont Corian
integral sink in Glacier
White
Tub: Trajet "LaStrata"
whirlpool in white
Toilet and Bidet:
American Standard
"Absolute" wall-hung
Shower Door: Basco ⅜"
frameless
Showerhead: Ondine
Shower faucets: Hansa
Sink faucets: Kohler
Vanity tops: Dupont
Corian in Glacier White
Lights: Progress
recessed hi-hats with
open trims and owner's
antique sconces
Drawer pulls: Hardware
Plus "Oriental" Series
Ventilation: Broan
exhaust/light combo
Shower walls: Dupont
Corian
**Valances and safety
bars:** Northern
Metalworks
In-floor heating: Warm
Floors

Arts and Crafts

THE ORIGINAL BATHROOM in this '50s-era home consisted
of poorly laid out cubicles. The lighting was inadequate,
and the space was hard to maintain. The homeowner, who
has multiple sclerosis, found it unsafe and nonfunctional.
Although she is ambulatory, the owner requested a space that
would address her special needs of fatigue, limited dexterity,
and sensitivity to noise and light. She emphasized that the
room should not appear institutional in any way. Her desire
was accessibility, function, and beauty.

Drawn to the Oriental influences within the Arts and
Crafts movement, she wanted to incorporate that style of
design as a showcase for a variety of antique accessories that
she had collected. Designer Rebecca Gullion Lindquist, of
Lindquist and Company, borrowed 2 feet of additional space
from an adjacent closet, making room for a whirlpool tub,
which she separated from a custom Corian shower with a
glass block wall. Minute attention was paid
to the aesthetic aspect of all accessibility
issues—from the sub-mounted tub under
a Corian deck to the custom-designed and
fabricated stainless-steel grab rails at the
tub, toilet, and bidet areas.

The completed room is a true reflection
of the Arts and Crafts era, with its natural
cherry cabinetry in the Craftsman style,
Oriental hardware, and the carefully
detailed moldings that frame the tile and
mirrored panels. «

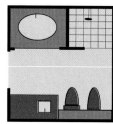

PHOTOGRAPHER: STEVE TIGGEMANN FOR JEFF FREY PHOTOGRAPHY

DESIGNER
Tim Koehler
Koehler Kitchen and Bath
1220-A Battleground Ave.
Greensboro, NC 27408
336-275-8402

SPECIAL FEATURES
Custom faux painting
and hand-painted
mural on walls; crystal
chandelier; plantation
shutters; beveled mirror;
custom ⅜" glass shower
enclosure

DIMENSIONS
14' x 11'

PRODUCTS USED
Tile: Verde Empress
Marble with bullnose
edge treatment
Cabinetry: Ultracraft
Greco
Mirrors: ¼" plate with
beveled edges
Sink: Undermount
Kohler porcelain
Tub: Whirlpool 72" x 42"
Venici with heater
Toilet: Kohler Wellington
white
Shower Door: custom
⅜" glass
Showerhead: Grohe
Pulsator in shower and
Kohler waterfall in tub
Sink Faucets: Kohler
Alterna
Shower Faucets: Grohe
body spray and hand-
held
Vanity Tops: Verde
Empress Marble
Lights: 8" recessed
can lights and antique
chandelier
Plumbing supplies: all
copper water pipes with
PVC drainlines
Drawer Pulls: Baldwin
Solid Brass Classic
**Towel Bars and Tissue
Holder:** Baldwin

Natural Wonders

WHAT HAPPENS when two dreamers meet a dream-maker?
Together they create an enchanted space with waterfalls,
tropical flowers, and birds that seem ready at any moment to
burst into song—a virtual symphony for the senses.

The homeowners have always loved their house in an old
established neighborhood of Greensboro, North Carolina.
They didn't want to move—ever. And yet they wanted a
larger and much more spectacular master bath and closet to
enhance its comfort. When they met Tim Koehler, owner of
Koehler Kitchen and Bath, their vision became a reality.

Koehler added a complete room to the back of the house.
The interior vaulted ceiling is divided into five different
planes converging beneath the peak of the outside hip. This
provides the perfect place for the antique chandelier.

Koehler set the tub in mud-based marble. However, code
demands required access to the electrical heater, so one of
the 12-inch marble squares is removable
and situated exactly in line with the
heater. The tub features a Kohler waterfall
faucet, while the shower displays myriad
handheld and body-spray faucets.

However, it is in the whimsical
and exotic interior decoration that the
homeowners allowed free rein to their
imaginations. Working with an artist, they
requested paintings of birds, butterflies,
flowers, and even frogs. This makes the
inside vista feel just like being outdoors. «

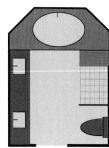

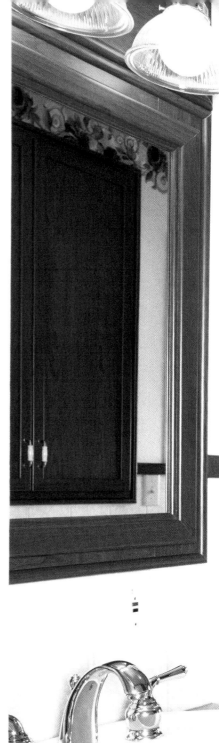

Abracadabra Bath

SOMETHING FROM NOTHING. A rabbit out of a hat. That's almost what was demanded when the homeowners decided to add a shower and cabinetry to a tiny bathroom. There just wasn't any space. Designer Mike Sohre, of Sohre's Kitchens & Baths, was asked to solve the problem. Major changes were required. The room was completely gutted and a closet space was appropriated to house the shower. Now working from the ground up, the Sohre's team transformed the closet into an elegant shower unit. All the things stored in the closet now could go into the custom cabinets above the stairwell. Formerly wasted space, it's now valuable. The new changes allowed room for a Roman tub, toilet, and vanity sink, all from the Kohler Portrait series.

To give the small room an open, elegant feeling, the window was enlarged and ceramic flooring installed. Matching wall tile, gold fixtures, and cherry cabinetry and trim complete the prestigious look. The finishing touches, so much appreciated by this tidy family, included an ADVent exhaust unit and a foot-operated pedal valve. All this without a magic wand! «

DESIGNER
Michael Sohre
Sohre's Kitchens & Baths
2125 Maryland Ave.
Sheboygan, WI 53081
920-458-0409

SPECIAL FEATURES
Custom vanity and medicine cabinet; linen cabinet built to utilize stairwell space; closet transformed into shower

DIMENSIONS
10' x 5'

PRODUCTS USED
Tile: Kate-Lo
Cabinetry: Sohre's custom cabinets with LaMica doors and Formica laminate
Sink(s): Kohler
Tub and toilet: Kohler Portrait Series
Shower Door: Showerite
Faucets: Moen
Vanity tops: Wilsonart
Lights: Task vanity light
Plumbing supplies: Glendale Supply
Drawer pulls: Cliffside
Ventilation: ADVent

PHOTOGRAPHER: PHILLIP HARSH

Limited Space?

THE HOME IS TRADITIONAL, located in an established, upscale neighborhood. But like most of their neighbors, these homeowners had a big problem—the 1950s bathrooms. The hall bathroom, in particular, was in need of major, immediate help.

Diana D. Mathews, CKD, and interior designer Shannon L. Saye were called to the rescue. They saw their challenges clearly: to transform a small, outdated room into an inviting, functional space for the couple's two daughters and guests. There was little square footage that could be utilized and a limited budget within which the homeowners could be comfortable.

The two girls needed individual space. To fill that need, the countertop space was extended on the available wall to house two sink basins. The preexisting wall mirror was framed with molding, and a cabinet was placed in the center. To add warmth to the space, the designers chose a new maple finish by Homecrest Cabinetry and selected several cabinet designs. Their magical manipulation included turning some of these cabinets upside-down and placing apothecary cabinets vertically to create storage space for the daughters' things. The cabinetry was designed to give the illusion of a piece of furniture, and drawer pulls were added in motifs of juniper leaves, butterflies, and flowers. «

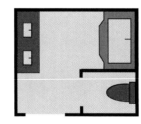

DESIGNER
Diana D. Mathews, CKD
Shannon L. Saye, interior designer
Distinctive Kitchens and Interiors
706 Edwardia Dr.
Greensboro, NC 27409
336-834-3131

SPECIAL FEATURES
Custom fluted molding encases the mirror and creates a backdrop for the vanity lights; apothecary drawers turned at an angle for storage; inverted sink bases for more drawer space

DIMENSIONS
8' x 9'

PRODUCTS USED
Tile: 8" square Lauflin Ceramic
Cabinetry: Homecrest
Showerhead: Delta Select
Sink Faucets: Barand
Shower Faucets: Delta Select
Vanity Tops: Cultured marble with custom bullnose edge
Lighting: Vanity by Minka, pendant light by Murray Feiss
Drawer Pulls: Cliffside Industries
Window Fabric: Fabricut
Rugs: Abu Oriental

A Narrow Escape

THIS SLEEK CONTEMPORARY BATH was part of a complete renovation. A second-floor commercial space was being converted into a luxury one-bedroom apartment. The space for the bathroom, however, was long and narrow—not quite 5 feet wide but a good 18 feet in length. Designer Michael C. Stockin came up with some strategies that not only use the allotted space to advantage but also result in a visually balanced composition.

Beneath the stairs leading to an upper floor, Stockin located the recessed whirlpool, forming an "L." The tub surround is high-gloss Avonite; to make a contrasting statement, the original old-brick surface was exposed.

At the other end of the bath a custom shower unit with Avonite walls and base was installed. Stockin used glass blocks to create a maze as the entrance to the shower blurring the visual boundaries of the room. Another trick of the eye is the diagonal arrangement of the floor tiles.

The two-toned custom cherry cabinets are echoed in the bedroom cabinetry, bringing unity to the master suite. Additional storage was created by building custom cabinets to fit in the space beneath the stairs. The tall custom-framed mirror with recessed shelf over the pedestal sink and the tall mirrors by the whirlpool work their own wonders at opening up the space. Brilliant design solutions result in a room where everything seems to be right in place. «

DESIGNER
Michael C. Stockin, CKD
Kuntriset Kitchens &
Baths Design Center
5127 State Highway 12
Norwich, NY 13815
607-336-4197

SPECIAL FEATURES
Custom-built shower with Avonite base and walls; sunken whirlpool with Avonite deck; custom recessed mirror with shelf.

DIMENSIONS
5' x 18'

PRODUCTS USED
Tile: Imola
Cabinetry: Wood Mode
Mirrors: Custom Avonite
Sink(s): Kohler Memoir Series
Tub: MTI
Toilet: Kohler Memoir Series
Showerhead: Kohler Revival Series
Sink and Shower Faucets: Kohler Revival Series
Lights: Task
Shower walls and base, whirlpool deck and custom mirror: Avonite Emerald Green Granite.

A Grand Scheme

PARENTS OF TWO DAUGHTERS, this Grandview, West Virginia, couple built a brand-new home to accommodate their ever-evolving needs. When they drew up the blueprints, one thing was for certain: they had to have a masterful master bathroom bedecked with an oversized walk-in shower. No small feat to design, the shower-sans-door plan called for a designer with an eye for detail and a knack for the creative. And that's why the husband and wife tasked Jeannie Richmond, of Interior Concepts, with the challenge.

Richmond's most daunting obstacle was figuring out how to fashion the shower within the confines of the space. Her solution: a curving creation ornamented with square glass blocks. Danny Burgess, of Great House Inc., brought the idea to fruition, adeptly constructing a sparkling structure that makes showering more of an artform than an ordinary daily ritual. Not only did he fashion the glass into a curving shape, but he also constructed a curved interior shower wall, which is festooned with a uniquely crafted tile pattern. His and her vanities give the couple their own spaces to prepare for the day, while walk-in closets adjoining the bathroom allow them ample space for their clothing and other storable items.

Beginning as a grandiose vision requiring an expert touch, the resulting room is an oasis boasting beauty that's crystal clear. «

DESIGNER
Jeannie Richmond
Interior Concepts
119 2nd St.
Beckley, WV 25801
304-255-6808

SPECIAL FEATURES
Circular glass block shower

DIMENSIONS
15' x 16'

PRODUCTS USED
Tile: Bedrosian travertine
Cabinetry: Holiday
Mirrors: Holiday frames
Sink(s): Classic marble
Toilet: Kohler
Vanity tops: Classic marble
Lights: Thomas Lighting
Plumbing supplies: Kohler
Drawer pulls: Top Knobs

MEMBER OF
SEN DESIGN GROUP

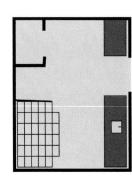

PHOTOGRAPHER: STEVE BRIGHTWELL

Bigger Bath

WHEN THE HOMEOWNERS moved back to their Virginia house after several years in California, they knew they had to do something with their tiny master bath and dressing area. The California house had allowed them a large, spacious bathroom with separate shower and whirlpool tub, a dry sauna, walk-in closets, and double vanity dressing area. Their Virginia accommodations were just too small.

Working with Steve Haught, of Kitchen Classics by Custom Crafters, Inc., the owners reconfigured their three-bedroom layout to make the two guest bedrooms a more comfortable size. The remaining space in the master suite sitting area was turned into a light-filled dressing room. This transformation made way for the former closets, dressing area and existing bath to be demolished and rebuilt into a dream bath.

Haught designed the custom double vanity with clipped cabinet corners and dressed the toe space with colonial base to create a furniture look. Kohler waterfall faucets removed countertop clutter.

The centerpiece for the remodel—the shower—was once the walk-in closet. The space was outfitted with dual thermostatic shower valves, volume controls, shower heads, six body sprays, a fold-down shower seat, and stream unit. A custom ¼-inch-thick clear-glass enclosure seals the shower for relaxing steam sessions but helps maintain the overall openness of the room. «

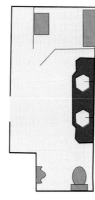

DESIGNER
Steven L. Haught
Kitchen Classics By
Custom Crafters Inc.
6023 Wilson Blvd.
Arlington, VA 22205
703-532-7000

SPECIAL FEATURES
Multi-person shower;
furniture-look cabinets;
three-piece wood and
tile crown molding;
urinal

DIMENSIONS
16'6'' x 8'

PRODUCTS USED
Tile: Thermae Caracalla
Cabinetry: Kountry Kraft
Mirrors: Robern
Sink(s): Kohler Terragon
Faucets: Kohler Falling
Water
Toilet: Kohler Memoirs
Stately
Urinal: Kohler Freshman
Shower Door: Phillips
Glass & Mirror (custom)
Showerhead: Kohler
Master Shower
Handheld Shower:
Kohler Master Shower
Body Sprays: Kohler
Master Shower
Shower Faucets: Kohler
Thermostatic Master
Shower
Vanity Tops: Silestone
Rosa Grey
Door/Drawer Hardware:
Siro
Steam Unit: Amerec
Floor Warming System:
Warmly Yours

Mini Masterpiece

WITH THE KIDS all grown and moved away, the empty-nester clients sought to remodel and add on to the bath in their traditional 1960s home. They charged Certified Remodeler Lee Thomas with giving them the luxury of a posh hotel bathroom within the confines of a small space.

The home is located on a large wooded lot, so the bathroom was redesigned to take advantage of the beautiful view of the backyard, lush with mature trees, a stream, and hills. To bring the outside in and let in lots of light, Thomas installed large circle-top windows on either side of the room and behind the whirlpool tub, which sits opposite the doorway and becomes a wonderful focal point.

His and her vanities were positioned on either side of the tub, allowing husband and wife to have a bit of private space. The wife's side also includes a sit-down makeup counter and the water closet. His side has a spacious 4-by-4 shower constructed of cultured marble.

The design was limited in width because the bathroom is located on the second story of the home and is connected to the adjacent master suite. In order to create a more open feeling, Thomas gave the room a vaulted ceiling, which, when combined with the rest of the improvements, gave this couple a bath that can take them comfortably into their golden years. «

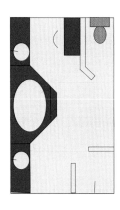

DESIGNER
Lee Thomas, CR
Signature Kitchen &
Baths by Lee Thomas
Construction
805 N. Main St.
North Canton, OH 44720
330-494-5455

SPECIAL FEATURES
4-by-4 angle
custom showers; his and
her vanities; makeup
counter

DIMENSIONS
9'6" x 16'8"

PRODUCTS USED
Tile: Florida
Cabinetry: Riviera
Sink(s): American
Marble Industries
Tub: MTI
Toilet: Barclay
Shower Door: Basco
Sink Faucets: Delta
Shower Faucets: Delta
Vanity Tops: American
Marble Industries
Lights: Task
Drawer Pulls: Amerock

PHOTOGRAPHER: STEVE WHITSITT

Quiet Sophistication

THE OWNERS OF THIS MOUNTAIN HOME, nestled in beautiful Breckenridge, Colorado, had a very distinct idea of how they wanted their new master bath to feel. They described their goal as "quiet sophistication," and they wanted the bathroom to complement their master bedroom. They also wished to have cabinetry that looked more like furniture than storage. The couple had one additional request: their beloved Yorkie, Zoey, needed a space all her own.

Linda Miller, of Aspen Grove Kitchen & Bath, Inc., worked with the couple to turn their vision into reality. Miller used cherry Bertch Legacy cabinets with rose stain and replaced the toekick with traditional turned feet. The result? A storage space that looks anything *but* utilitarian. The light fixtures, faucets, and accessories have a muted silver finish, adding a soft glimmer to the room, and the Porcher "Draped" sinks soften the look of the granite countertops. These small touches provide the sophisticated style the owners desired. A deck-mounted jetted tub and a dual steam shower with his and her shower-heads provide the ultimate in relaxation.

Last, but certainly not least, Miller created a space for Zoey by installing two knee drawers stacked just below the countertop. The final result is a calm, inviting bathroom where everyone in the family can come to relax. «

DESIGNER
Linda G. Miller
Aspen Grove Kitchen &
Bath, Inc.
P.O. Box 860
975 N. Ten Mile Drive, #E1
Frisco, CO 80443
970-468-5393

SPECIAL FEATURES
His and her sinks and storage; turned-feet accents to create furniture look; specially designed space for dog

DIMENSIONS
11' x 18'

PRODUCTS USED
Cabinetry: Bertch Legacy
Sink: Porcher
Vanity Tops: Granite
Lights: Kichler
Drawer Pulls: Bertch Legacy

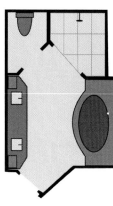

PHOTOGRAPHER: MATTHEW L. KRANE

Rejuvenated Retreat

THE HOMEOWNERS of this circa-1980 almond-tiled bathroom needed more from the room than what it was providing. They desired a spot where they could retreat after a long day to rejuvenate their minds and bodies. The couple teamed up with Jeff Boico, of Classic Kitchen and Bath Center Ltd., who helped to transform their bathroom.

The homeowners wanted many conveniences in their bathroom, which meant Boico had the challenge of integrating all the desired components while still maintaining a unified look. The homeowners requested a TV, which Boico hid in a corner-angled unit. They also wanted a refrigerator in the bathroom, so Boico installed a base fridge with cabinet panels that blend in beautifully. The couple also desired his and her amenities, so the designer made the shower larger to accommodate two people and installed the two-person whirlpool tub and two sinks the homeowners desired.

Together, the homeowners and the designer chose light butter-cream colors and architectural details such as columns and hand-carved onlays. The transfigured room is now a space where both homeowners can comfortably relax and wash the day away. «

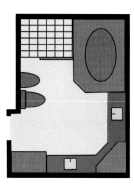

DESIGNER
Jeff Boico
Classic Kitchen and Bath
Center Ltd.
1052 Northern Blvd.
Roslyn, NY 11576
516-621-7700

SPECIAL FEATURES
Hidden flat-screen TV; integrated refrigerator drawers; whirlpool tub; shower for two; hand carving; columns; furniture detail on the cabinetry; hand-painted, glazed finish

DIMENSIONS
12' x 15'

PRODUCTS USED
Tile: Crema Marfil with Empress Verde Dot
Cabinetry: Custom
Sink: Kohler
Tub: Kohler
Toilet: Kohler
Bidet: Kohler
Shower Door: Custom
Refrigerator: Sub-Zero
Faucets: Santec
Refrigerator: Sub-Zero

PHOTOGRAPHER: STEVEN PAUL WHITSITT

Practical Beauty

OPPOSITES ATTRACT, and that fact is evident in this stunning bathroom. As the homeowners planned their new house, they knew what they wanted from their master bath: a visually fascinating room that reflected the architecture of the house, while maintaining a high level of practicality.

Dennis Regole, CKD, of Charlestowne Kitchen & Bath, set out to make this vision a reality. Regole designed arched mirrors with detailed casing, surrounded by dark cherry woods. The style of the mirrors complements the beautiful Palladian windows located throughout the rest of the home. Regole placed 12 beaded pilasters on various corners of the bathroom, creating a look of architectural stability. An attractive island balances the height of the tall ceiling. Just as functional as it is beautiful, the island has deep drawer storage for towels that opens toward the tub.

Regole wanted to be sure he blended beauty into function, thus achieving the attractive yet practical space the homeowners desired. He used limestone for the floor in order to minimize slippage. He also disguised the numerous electrical outlets in the marble backsplashes and designed the walk-in shower sans door for ease of cleaning. Regole even installed electrically controlled blinds for privacy. The end result is a breathtaking bathroom that makes life in this Midwest home practically perfect. «

DESIGNER
Dennis M. Regole CKD
Charlestowne Kitchen
& Bath
1519 E. Main St.
St. Charles, IL 60174
630-377-7878 x 137

SPECIAL FEATURES
Center island with indirect lighting at toe kick; 10-foot ceiling with 12-foot coffered tray; painted columns and wainscot panels at tub deck; walk-in shower with bench and glass block

DIMENSIONS
14' x 18'

PRODUCTS USED
Tile: Luna Limestone
Cabinetry: Crystal Cabinet Works, Woodbury and Wheaton Cherry with black highlights
Sink: Kohler
Tub: Kohler
Toilet: Kohler
Vanity Tops: Marble
Plumbing Supplies: Giagni; Grohe (shower)
Drawer Pulls: Omnia
Shower Room: Luma Limestone
Floors: Honed Luma Limestone
Floor Perimeter Around Island: Polished Luna Limestone

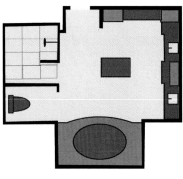

Classic Beauty

THIS REMARKABLE 90-YEAR-OLD HOME is located in the beautiful Chapel Hill Historic District in North Carolina. Bill Cederberg, of Cederberg Kitchens & Additions, was hired to update the master bath of this beautifully preserved house. The owners love their historic home, but they still desired modern conveniences such as extra storage space and a larger area in which to move about.

Cederberg's task was to transform the bath into a more spacious and functional room while maintaining consistency with the architecture of the house. Not only did he have to earn the homeowners' approval, but any changes he made had to be approved by the Chapel Hill Historic Society.

The new layout of the master bathroom included a 10-foot-high ceiling and a large walk-in closet with plenty of storage. The tub was placed beneath the triple windows, while a large shower with a frameless glass enclosure was tucked into a recess on the interior wall. To enhance the spacious feeling of the room, Cederberg installed an impressive 8-foot double vanity. The end result of the remodel is an elegant room that celebrates classic appeal, as well as modern design. «

DESIGNER
William A. Cederberg
Cederberg Kitchens &
Additions
630 Weaver Dairy Road,
Suite 106
Chapel Hill, NC 27514
919-967-1171

SPECIAL FEATURES
White enamel inset door

DIMENSIONS
16' x 10'

PRODUCTS USED
Tile: Carerra Marble
Cabinetry: Cuisine
Cabico
Sink: Kohler
Vanity Tops: Carerra
marble
Lighting: Seagull
Drawer Pulls: Top Knobs

PHOTOGRAPHER: SETH TICE LEWIS

Historical Home

THIS ARTISAN-BUILT RESIDENCE is a house with a rich history. It was built during the time when California's classic Bay Bridge was under construction. During this period, all of the building trades went on strike. As a result, European artisans were brought in to finish constructing the home. The artisans' fine craftsmanship is apparent in the uncommon attention to detail in every aspect of the house, such as handmade tiles and hand-hewn timbers in the ceiling. So when the homeowners decided to remodel the bathroom, they needed someone who could match the quality of the previous work.

Marilyn Gardunio and the design team at J.B. Turner & Sons were equipped for the challenge, with Gardunio's husband, John, and son, Sean, serving as master craftsmen. The home features a 1930s Mediterranean look, and the design team matched the theme with fine plaster on the walls and custom-made windows. For modern convenience, Gardunio implemented a therapeutic spa bath, which includes such amenities as body sprays, a steam shower, and a custom shower seat. Other conveniences include towel warmers and radiant-heat flooring.

The new bathroom is a beautiful extension of the original house. The owners now have a retreat where they can enjoy the beauty of the past and the luxury of the present. «

DESIGNER
Marilyn C. Gardunio CKD
J.B. Turner & Sons
3911 Piedmont Ave.
Oakland, CA 94611
510-658-3441

SPECIAL FEATURES
Concealed toilet; body sprays and custom seat in shower; radiant flooring

DIMENSIONS
8' x 10'

PRODUCTS USED
Tile: Tile Shop; Ann Sacks
Cabinetry: Jay Rambo
Mirrors: Robern
Sink: Kohler
Window: Custom
Toilet: Kohler
Shower Door: Custom
Vanity Tops: Caesarstone
Lights: Piedmont
Plumbing Supplies: Grohe
Drawer Pulls: LB Brass
Floor: Warmly Yours
Towel Warmer: Zephyr
Steam Mist: Ginger

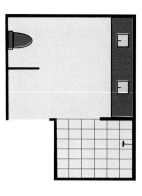

PHOTOGRAPHER: STEVEN PAUL WHITSITT

Tranquil Retreat

Owned by a young couple who purchased the home after the original owners sold it, the master bath inside this Flanders, New Jersey, dwelling needed a radical renovation. To transform the dull white room into a tranquil, traditional retreat, the homeowners called on the husband and wife team at Zehnbauer's Construction, a couple to whom they'd turned in the past for various remodeling tasks.

The design team's assignment: to enlarge the shower, reduce the size of the tub, and add a general sense of relaxing ambiance to the room. Most challenging was the process of how to aesthetically incorporate access to the whirlpool pump. Putting his creativity to work, Ron Zehnbauer designed a removable tile panel that hides the motor while allowing the homeowners access to it should they need to perform maintenance-related tasks.

Diane Zehnbauer worked closely with the homeowners to help achieve their desired aesthetic. More specifically, when the lady of the home selected her tiles of choice from Specialty Tile, Diane assisted her in creating an arrangement to best suit the room. The finished space is a clean-lined oasis with a traditional flair. «

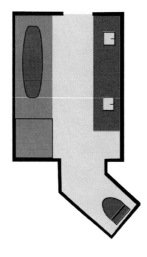

DESIGNER
Diane Zehnbauer
Zehnbauer's
Construction LLC
180 Gold Mine Road
Flanders, NJ 07885
973-442-7844

SPECIAL FEATURES
Tile arranged in a brick pattern; removable tile panel to disguise whirlpool pump

DIMENSIONS
10' x 9' (main)
4' x 3' (water closet)

PRODUCTS USED
Tile: Alabaster Miami Beige; ⅛ Pompei; 1 x 12 Pencil
Cabinetry: Bertch Tiffany
Mirrors: Bertch
Sink(s): Kohler Devonshire Bisque
Tub: Kohler
Toilet: Toto Clayton
Shower door: Semi-frameless
Lights: Bertch traditional light bar
Drawer pulls: Bertch

MEMBER OF
SEN DESIGN GROUP

PHOTOGRAPHER: MARC SCHWARTZ, CELEBRATIONS STUDIOS

It's in the Details

THIS BATH BOASTS A VARIETY OF DETAILS designed to create a host of simple pleasures. Elegant fixtures gleam with a chrome finish, and tile in a soothing neutral hue complements the crisp white countertop and shower bench. Designer Michael O'Connor and decorator Ann Weigel, of Signature Kitchens and Baths of Sarasota, selected each item with care in an effort to create the spa-like ambiance the homeowners desired. Whether it was the quest for the ideal towel hook or the installation of cabinetry that seems to float in the air, not a single detail was overlooked.

The tall cabinets, which flank the vanity and stand as silent guards of the peaceful Zen retreat, disguise their functionality. Inside, each cabinet is filled with drawers and shelves containing a linen closet, electrical outlets, and makeup organizers.

O'Connor designed the shower for organization—his and her cubbies are a great place to stash necessities—and as a place to unwind and release the stresses of the day. Three body sprays, a showerhead, and a handheld showerhead top off the tranquil oasis. From within the shower, the reeded glass above the bench adds another visual element, with its strong vertical lines that mimic those in the cabinets and provide a sense of privacy for the toilet and bidet. Such details create indulgent pleasures. «

DESIGNER
Michael O'Connor
Signature Kitchens and
Baths of Sarasota
6528 S. Tamiami Trail
Sarasota, FL 34231
941-894-6692

SPECIAL FEATURES
Tall cabinetry that appears to float above the floor; elegant fixtures; body sprays; handheld showerhead

DIMENSIONS
12' x 13'

PRODUCTS USED
Tile: Daltile Veranda Body Gravel
Cabinetry: Custom natural wenge
Sink(s): American Standard Studio undermount
Toilet: Toto Pacifica
Shower door: Quality enclosures, ⅜-inch
Vanity tops: Caesarstone Blizzard
Lights: Ginger Double Large Rosette
Plumbing supplies: Hansgrohe; Axor/Starck; Grohe
Drawer pulls: Dekkor
Bidet: Toto Pacifica

MEMBER OF

SEN DESIGN GROUP

PHOTOGRAPHER: GENE POLLUX

Tuscan Oasis

Stuck in the '80s, this master bathroom boasted an enviable amount of square footage but had dated oak cabinetry and white tile. Furthermore, the shower stall was in the corner with two large windows, blocking light into the space. To solve this design dilemma, Christine Marks, of Kitchen Places, came to the homeowners' rescue.

Marks swapped the jetted bath and shower. The new shower features his and her body sprays, shampoo niches, a bench and interior window niches to prevent a cave-like feel. While the basic design was relatively easy, the finish selection was challenging. Marks opted to complement the homeowners' strong design sense with dramatic colors and Tuscan finishes: tumbled-marble tiles mixed with tumbled-glass tiles, granite countertops, and Lyptus wood cabinets.

Because the finishes can be cold, Marks installed an in-floor tile warming system and pivoting heated towel rack to ensure warmth. The ancillary rooms include a water closet with a bidet and extra storage. A dressing area connects to the walk-in closet and shares the Tuscan motif with the use of a window seat and barrel-vaulted ceiling. Finishing touches include crystal and bead light fixtures, custom art glass windows, and oil-rubbed bronze hardware. The finished result is a Tuscan oasis in the midst of California. «

DESIGNER
Christine A. Marks
Kitchen Places
4125 Market St., #1
Ventura, CA 93003
805-658-0440

SPECIAL FEATURES
His and her shower and vanities; art glass windows; custom arched mirrors and wood frames

DIMENSIONS
16' x 16'

PRODUCTS USED
Tile: Tumbled travertine, glass mosaic inserts
Cabinetry: DuraSupreme
Mirror: Custom arched
Sink(s): Kohler
Tub: Jason Hydrotherapy
Toilet: Kohler
Shower door: Custom arched, frameless
Vanity tops: Giallo Atlantide granite
Lights: Wilshire Apprezzare Collection
Plumbing supplies: Rohl, Grohe
Drawer pulls: Tob Knobs
In-floor heat: Warmly Yours
Towel warmer: WarmaTowel

MEMBER OF
SEN DESIGN GROUP

PHOTOGRAPHER: STEVEN PAUL WHITSITT

Innovative Angle

FACED WITH A BORING BATHROOM PALETTE and a vacant whirlpool tub, the owners of this Naperville, Illinois, master bath knew it was time for a remodel. With all of the design challenges that lay before them, the homeowners were overwhelmed, to say the least. But after hearing a proposed solution from their designer, Jessica A. Gomes, of Casa Bella Design Center, the owners knew they'd have their dream room after all.

Gomes based her plan on an innovative use of angles, which is evident in the out-of-the-box design scheme. An angled tub deck helps enlarge the shower space, while the angled entry and frameless enclosure add aesthetic interest. Two recessed niches and a shower seat lend functionality to the room's flair. Gomes continued the angled theme by crafting a custom his and her vanity areas featuring a large central linen cabinet.

To complete the look, the designer installed cool blue tile to contrast with the warm cherry cabinets. The vanity area sports a custom tiled-mirror treatment with floating light fixtures to reflect the room's soothing colors and light. Chrome plumbing and accessories add sparkle. With its carefully crafted concept, Casa Bella delivered a design that met and exceeded the homeowners' expectations. «

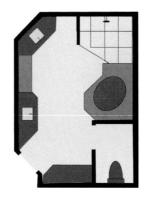

DESIGNER
Jessica A. Gomes
Casa Bella Design Center
15 W. Jefferson, Suite 103
Naperville, IL 60540
630-718-1440

SPECIAL FEATURES
Angled tub placement;
waterfall; framed mosaic
tile insert; angled
custom cabinetry layout;
tile-framed mirrors

DIMENSIONS
15' x 11'

PRODUCTS USED
Tile: Alfa Ceramiche
Nepal Sanjani with
accents
Cabinetry: Ultracraft
Destiny Shaker Wide
Cherry
Mirrors: Custom
frameless installation
Sink(s): Kohler Caxton
undermount
Tub: MTI Whirlpool
Toilet: Kohler Cimarron
Shower door: Custom
frameless enclosure
Vanity tops: Atlantic
black granite
Lights: Ginger Surface
Collection
Plumbing supplies:
Danze Parmaline in
chrome
Drawer pulls:
Dekkor chrome
Other:
Zehnder towel radiator

MEMBER OF
SEN DESIGN GROUP

PHOTOGRAPHER: SHERMAN DUNHAM

Cozy in Colorado

DESIGNER
Nancy Woodka
Columbine Kitchen
& Bath
309 3rd St.
Castle Rock, CO 80104
303-688-4199

SPECIAL FEATURES
Custom color palette;
in-floor radiant heating;
steam shower with
frameless doors

DIMENSIONS
10' x 18'

PRODUCTS USED
Tile: Bedrosian
Contempo, Grey; Jeffrey
Court, Sonoma Current
Cabinetry: Medallion,
Glenwood slab door in
cherry with wheat finish
Mirrors: Binswanger
Glass Co.
Sink: Frosted glass
vessels from Kubel
Distributing
Tub: American Standard
Toilet: American
Standard
Shower door: Frameless
Vanity tops: Silestone
Lighting: Kichler fixture
Plumbing supplies:
Kubel Distributing
Drawer pulls: Dekkor
**Radiant in-floor
heating:** Warmly Yours

MEMBER OF
SEN DESIGN GROUP

WHEN THE OWNER of this 10-year-old Castle Rock, Colorado, home wished to expand the master bath, designers Trish Boylan, of Boylan Design Group, and Nancy Woodka, of Columbine Kitchen & Bath, agreed to the challenge. Their task: to enlarge the space and design a contemporary aesthetic consistent with the owner's love of modern design.

To evoke a soothing ambiance, Boylan suggested a gray and lavender color palette. The designers adorned the floor and the lower half of the wall with Bedrosian porcelain tiles; listello mosaic with glass squares in a variety of fresh berry colors adorns the remaining wall surface. Lavender and silver faux paint complete the space. Cherry Medallion cabinetry with a wheat finish adds a sense of warmth, while the Glenwood slab door evokes a modern aesthetic. Because the room lacked a long row of vanity cabinets, Woodka recommended varying the height and depth of the center drawer section for visual appeal. She also suggested rectangular vessel sinks to reflect the shape in the block glass window. Silestone's Leather Look Gray Amazon dresses the countertops.

Luxurious elements include a steam shower (converted from the original), Warmly Yours radiant in-floor heating, and an American Standard whirlpool for indulgent soaks. The remodeled master bath is a cozy retreat in the heart of Colorado. «

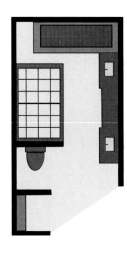

PHOTOGRAPHER: TED SPRING

Pure Tranquility

WHEN FACED WITH THE CHALLENGE of transforming a dated, sunken tile tub/shower combination bathroom into a luxurious master bath, this homeowner researched her options and zeroed in on a previously published project by Karen Bieszczak, of Bzak Design Group. Though the homeowner desired to duplicate the published project to fit her space, Bieszczak knew the design needed to be unique. She also knew it should represent the character of the individual home and the lifestyle of the homeowners.

To begin the project, Bieszczak took an inventory of personal toiletries and examined the closet space requirements, which would end up dictating the actual square footage needed for the addition. Upon completing these preliminaries, she conceded that the original design would not accommodate the homeowners' storage needs. As a result, the project was put on hold for a year to increase the investment so as to maintain the integrity of the design. This extra time gave Bieszczak and her clients a more relaxed schedule for product selection, which ensured optimal quality and value while maintaining the goal of selecting rich materials that give the feeling of touching velvet, silk, and satin. At the end of the day, this couple now finds themselves retreating to their master suite to enjoy pure relaxation. «

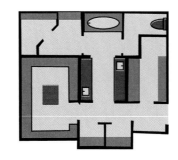

DESIGNER
Karen A. Bieszczak, CKD
Bzak Design Group
614 Wooster Pike, Suite 3
Terrace Park, OH 45174
513-831-3155

SPECIAL FEATURES
Mirrored closet doors to visually expand the space; generous use of marble; rich color palette

DIMENSIONS
17' x 20'

PRODUCTS USED
Tile: Dark Empador marble
Cabinetry: Holiday Newcastle Maple Country Hearth
Mirrors: Basco
Sink(s): Kohler
Tub: Jacuzzi
Toilet: Toto
Shower Door: Basco
Showerhead: Kohler
Sink Faucets: Kohler
Vanity Tops: Dark Empador marble
Lights: Central
Drawer Pulls: Top Knobs

PHOTOGRAPHER: DAVID STEINBRUNNER

Seascape Fantasy

TO CREATE THIS UNDER-THE-SEA BATHROOM, the homeowner called on Rahnee Gladwin, of R. Gladwin i. Design–Tile, to create a space that might capture the sense of excitement associated with a deep-sea dive. To achieve her client's dream, Gladwin utilized mosaic art to create a room reminiscent of a tropical reef. A large-scale, freestanding mosaic wall with a floating sea turtle is perhaps the pièce de résistance. Furthering the mosaic theme, a bonefish and crab skirt the tub. The handcrafted mosaic incorporates 86 colors of polished, matte, opaque, and iridescent ceramic and glass, as well as 15 colors of tumbled and polished stone. Oceanside Glasstile Tessera clads the surrounding walls, custom tub interior, and reverse side of the mosaic wall.

The floor of the wet area boasts Jerusalem gold-tumbled-stone mosaic and is topped with a ceiling composed of matte glass tiles. Chassagne-beige honed French limestone composes the floor and countertops of the vanity area, as well as the slab for the tub deck.

Also of interest is the showerhead, which is identified as a water feature. The Dornbracht Rain Sky was imported from Germany and is said to be the first of its type imported to the United States in 2006. In the end, the client was more than satisfied with the stunning creation and the accurate portrayal of the colors and forms of sea life. «

DESIGNER
Rhanee Gladwin
R. Gladwin i. Design–Tile
408 Water Street
Kerrville, TX 75028
830-257-6088

SPECIAL FEATURES
Master bath with a large wet area containing an open shower and custom tub; large-scale mosaic wall with return and seat

DIMENSIONS
16' x 14'

PRODUCTS USED
Cabinets: Custom, burled elm with birdseye maple banding
Flooring: Chassagne beige honed French limestone (vanity); tumbled Jerusalem gold limestone (wet area)
Countertops: Chassagne beige honed French limestone
Faucets: Dornbracht Terra
Showerhead: Dornbracht Rain Sky
Lighting: Recessed
Drawer pulls: Foundry Art, Cabochon in traditional bronze

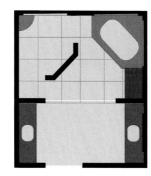

Expanded Estate

SITUATED IN BUDA, TEXAS, the owners of this home desired to transform the original 1,500-square-foot starter residence for a childless newlywed couple into an estate suited for a family of six. To achieve the task, they called on Stewart Davis, of CG&S Design-Build. Davis renovated the entire dwelling, greatly enlarging the space and giving it a comprehensive facelift. Among its most beautiful features, the bath areas rank at the top of the list.

Within the master bath, Davis evoked a go-for-it design featuring soft colors and intricate details. The room sits beneath a barrel-vaulted ceiling lit by cable lights. Predominant features include a seamless walk-in shower for two and a curvy seat, as well as a central jetted tub for two. The bath boasts a generous toilet niche and a vanity wall large enough for the couple to share. The shower and toilet spaces are shielded from direct view but remain open and connected with the central glass block partition, creating subtle division among tub, shower, and toilet space.

The expansive windows usher in ample daylight, providing an extra glow. The bath has a strategic design that allows for maximum use of abundant storage space. The curves displayed in the bathroom add character to the overall visual and fit well with the theme of softness and water. The result of this master bath remodel left the couple delighted and in anxious anticipation of the additional two bath remodels. «

DESIGNER
Stewart Davis
CG&S Design-Build
402 Corral Lane
Austin, TX 78745
512-444-1580

SPECIAL FEATURES
Varying ceiling heights;
glass partition

DIMENSIONS
14' x 14'

PRODUCTS USED
Cabinetry: Amazonia
Custom Cabinetry,
painted
Countertops: Tropical
Green granite
Sink(s): Proflo, Ferguson
Faucet(s): Moen
Tub: Pearle
Toilet: Toto, Ferguson;
Carusoe, white
Shower fittings: Moen
Flooring: Stained
concrete, jagger scored
Cable lighting: Tech
Lighting
**Downlights, accent
lights:** Juno Lighting

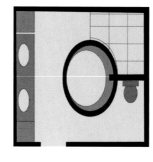

Fit for a Princess

LOCATED IN A BUDA, TEXAS, ESTATE, this bath is part of an addition to the dwelling specifically designed to house the children. This particular bath was especially created for the homeowner's only daughter, the sister of three brothers. As such, the girl's parents wanted her to have a bathroom all her own, a feminine space where she could escape from her boys-will-be-boys siblings.

Lavender and light blues pervade the space and provide a soft child-friendly atmosphere that will not outgrow the child as time passes. The clean, colorful, simple feel of the room allows for creative versatility. Concrete floors, laminate countertops, tiled showers, and painted cabinets provide an economical solution for beauty, durability, and easy maintenance.

To provide a warm atmosphere and maximize the use of installed lighting, designer Stewart Davis dropped the ceiling perimeter lower than the central area. Windows and Juno light fixtures usher ample light into the space. The end result is a feminine bathroom designed to give a young girl a haven away from her three brothers, as well as an economical option for her parents. «

DESIGNER
Stewart Davis
CG&S Design-Build
402 Corral Lane
Austin, TX 78745
512-444-1580

SPECIAL FEATURES
Lower ceilings around perimeter

DIMENSIONS
5' x 10'

PRODUCTS USED
Cabinetry: Amazonia custom cabinetry, painted
Tub: Kohler
Vanity: Wilsonart laminate
Basin: Proflo
Faucets: Moen
Shower fittings: Moen
Flooring: Stained concrete, jagger scored
Toilet: Toto, Carusoe, white
Lighting: Juno

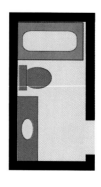

Boys Will Be Boys

THE LAST OF THREE BATHROOM REMODELS, this renovation was to suit three boys. Designed by Stewart Davis, of CG&S Design-Build, the bathroom boasts an environment suitable for the wear and tear that typically accompanies male children. And similar to their sister's bathroom, the brothers' space is located in the children's section of this Texas home, thus providing the youngest members of the family with a place to call their own.

In an effort to warrant the room durable and easy to clean, Stewart selected concrete, plastic laminate, and tile as the materials of choice. To create a sense of energetic zeal and to add a splash of color, Davis designed a fun-filled tile pattern. He also arranged the room into three separate zones. By creating a separate shower, toilet, and vanity space, the bathroom can effectively accommodate the concurrent occupation of three boys. The shower, strategically placed in the corner of the room, maximizes the area and eliminates dead space. To accommodate the young residents' belongings, Stewart incorporated an array of ample storage space. The completed room is now an area suitable for the rambunctious energy that is often associated with a brood of young boys. «

DESIGNER
Stewart Davis
CG&S Design-Build
402 Corral Lane
Austin, TX 78745
512-444-1580

SPECIAL FEATURES
Lower ceilings around perimeter

DIMENSIONS
12' x 6'6"

PRODUCTS USED
Cabinetry: Amazonia custom cabinetry, painted
Sink(s): Proflo
Faucet(s): Moen
Tub: Kohler
Vanity: Wilsonart laminate
Shower fittings: Moen
Flooring: Stained concrete, jagger scored
Toilet: Toto, Carusoe, white
Lighting: Juno

Modern Ranch

THIS INTERIOR BATH is located inside a getaway home that boasts a modern ranch aesthetic. Designed by David Webber, of Webber + Studio Inc., the bathroom is intended to accommodate multiple guests at once. As such, Webber opted to separate the vanity and toilet areas. In an effort to allow multiple users within the space, he also decided to construct double sinks.

Nestled between a mud room and a main hallway, the room has virtually no windows to the outside. Thus, the only natural light that seeps into the space is the light that finds its way in from the mud room. A small window between the mud room and the vanity area ushers in just the right amount of sunlight, while also providing a sense of necessary privacy. Mesquite cabinets lined with steel-edge banding warm the space. The cabinetry was custom designed by Archwood Custom Cabinets. Following the completion of the project, the homeowners stated that they wished their Florida home was as much fun as their ranch-themed Texas haven. «

DESIGNER
Webber + Studio Inc.
300 West Ave., Suite 1322
Austin, TX 78701
512-236-1032

SPECIAL FEATURES
Mesquite cabinetry
with steel band;
red travertine for
countertops and tiles

DIMENSIONS
6' x 10' (vanity);
6' x 7' (bath)

PRODUCTS USED
Cabinetry: Archwood
Custom Cabinets
Flooring: Custom pecan
Countertops: Marble,
Architectural Tile and
Stone
Lighting: Custom by
Two Hills Studio
Sinks: Water Works
and Rocky Mountain
hardware
Wallcovering: Red
travertine tile and
plaster
Cabinetry: Mesquite

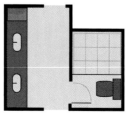

Lavish Lighting

In the midst of a remodel, this Austin, Texas, homeowner opted to extend the size of her home in an effort to give her the ability to create an entirely new master bath area. The task went to Al York, Heather McKinney, and Will Wood at McKinney Architects. When the architects began the project, they knew natural light was an important component to be included in the bath. The adjacent home, however, rendered the windows on one wall virtually functionless. So to usher in as much natural sunlight as possible, the team installed a skylight above the tub and shower, which adds an exceptional alternative to the bank of blocked windows.

Because the owner desired a bathroom that would be simple to navigate, another key feature in the room was circulation. Thus, the architects arranged a walk-in shower to complement the tub, which is set against the wall; both fixtures strategically project the elements into the space. This not only creates a highly functional layout, but omits clutter as well. The glass wall dividing the tub from the shower also creates an opportunity for maximum natural lighting. In the end, satisfaction abounded within the new space. «

DESIGNER
Al York, Heather McKinney, Will Wood
McKinney Architects, Inc.
297 W. Eighth St.
Austin, TX 78701
512-476-0201

SPECIAL FEATURES
Shower/tub combo

DIMENSIONS
12' x 15'

PRODUCTS USED
Casework: Painted
Sinks: Kohler
Tub: Duravit Happy D
Vanity tops: Honed Slate

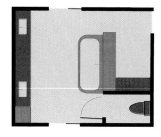

PHOTOGRAPHER: GREG HURSLEY

Zen-Inspired Space

OWNED BY A SMALL FAMILY, which includes the parents and two kids, this home exudes a sense of welcoming warmth. Such was the emotion the homeowners also desired in their new master bathroom. To create their dream design, the couple tapped David Webber, of Webber + Studio, Inc.

Among their desires, the couple wanted something elegant with an Asian influence. To create a Zen-inspired space, Webber incorporated substantial amounts of limestone and mahogany hardwood. He also integrated a mahogany surround for the bathtub and countertops; the rich mahogany complements the oak cabinetry. A large window overlooking an outside garden space furthers the Zen ambiance. Pocket doors with translucent glass provide a sense of separation between the bathroom and its adjoining room.

Additionally, the room boasts an open-air pavilion-like quality, enhanced by the large window, which opens the space to the outdoors. High-end fixtures and fittings, including a Duravit sink and a Kohler tub, top off the space. The result is a master bath that serves as a private retreat where the couple can go to relax and get away from it all. «

DESIGNER
David Webber
Webber + Studio Inc.
300 West Ave., Ste. 1322
Austin, TX 78701
512-236-1032

SPECIAL FEATURES
Mahogany tub surround; high-end fixtures; view overlooking the garden outside

DIMENSIONS
9' x 20'

PRODUCTS USED
Tile: Leuders limestone
Cabinetry: Oak
Sinks: Duravit
Tub: Kohler
Toilet: Kohler
Vanity tops: Custom mahogany
Lights: Prandina
Plumbing supplies: Hansgrohe, Kohler
Drawer pulls: Hafele

PHOTOGRAPHER: TOM MCCONNELL

Mid-Century Serenity

WHEN FACED WITH THE DESIRE TO REMODEL THIS HOME, these homeowners tasked Kevin Alter and Keune Shawn Peter, of Alterstudio Architects, LLP, with the challenge of totally gutting and renovating the bath area. As a professional couple with grown children, the homeowners wanted a design that might allow their tastes and personalities to shine through the remodel. Though they originally preferred traditional styling, they have since gained appreciation for mid-century modern architecture and furniture.

With stunning views of the landscape beyond, the designers designated the outside views as the focal point of the room. Floor-to-ceiling glass doors, which take the place of a formerly opaque wall, serve as the room's highlight. Bringing style and interest to the room is a floating vanity, as well as an ipe bench in the shower supported by glass on one side and steel on the other. The completed project is best defined as clean, modern, and bright; it is a bathroom that perfectly suits the homeowners' taste. Several months after the completion of their new design, the couple is still amazed at the positive impact the room makes on them each day. «

DESIGNER
Kevin Alter,
Keune Shawn Peter
Alterstudio Architects LLP
1403 Rio Grande St.
Austin, TX 78701
512-499-8007

SPECIAL FEATURES
Floor-to-ceiling sliding glass; cherry vanity; ipe bench in shower

DIMENSIONS
10' x 12'

PRODUCTS USED
Tile: Leuders limestone
Cabinetry: Custom cherry
Mirrors: Custom
Shower door: Custom, frameless
Faucet: Dornbracht Tara Classic
Shower hardware: Danze
Benches: Custom cherry

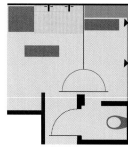

Texas Tudor

DESIGNED BY MARK CRAVOTTA, of Cravotta Studios, this Texas bathroom boasts an array of features that make it both a beautiful creation and an ultra-luxurious escape. Though it features a fairly simple design, Cravotta's biggest challenge was installing the flooring and the wainscoting. The difficulty was due to the fact that the materials for both were not traditional tiles. Instead, Cravotta used white Calcutta-gold marble slabs measuring 4 square feet and 3 centimeters thick. Beneath the floor, he also installed an in-floor heating system, which was specially crafted to work with the thickness of the material atop it.

A variety of additional luxuries is located throughout the room. Featuring an array of 12 body jets, the shower is an indulgent delight. A custom-crafted mirror conceals a plasma TV. When turned off, the television monitor disappears into the mirrored surface. Custom Biedermeier vanity cabinets provide a stunning addition to the room. And a built-in espresso machine, a refrigerator, and a bar assure the homeowners that everything they need to relax is at their fingertips. The room is reminiscent of a bath suite one might find in the finest of ninteenth century European hotels. Ideally suited for this small Texas family, the room is a beautiful creation that caused the homeowners tears of joy upon first sight. «

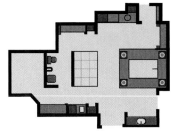

DESIGNER
Mark Cravotta
Cravotta Studios
3601 S. Congress Ave.,
Building C
Austin, TX 78704
512-499-0400

SPECIAL FEATURES
Custom mirror with plasma TV; custom Biedermeier vanity cabinets; built-in espresso machine, refrigerator, and bar

DIMENSIONS
20' x 18'

PRODUCTS USED
Tile: Calcutta Gold marble slab
Cabinetry: Custom Biedermeier reproduction
Mirrors: Custom
Sinks: Waterworks
Toilet: Toto
Vanity tops: Custom onyx
Lights: Antique fixture
Cabinet hardware: Alexander Merchant Specialty Hardware

Curves and Candor

DESIGNER
Mark Cravotta
Cravotta Studios
3601 S. Congress Ave.,
Building C
Austin, TX 78704
512-499-0400

SPECIAL FEATURES
Curved cabinets,
shower; glass
countertops; hand-hewn
flooring

DIMENSIONS
12' x 18'

PRODUCTS USED
Tile: Architerra
Cabinetry: Custom
beachwood by Kevin
Coy
Sinks: Vitraform
integrated sinks,
countertops
Tub: Pearl
Toilet: Toto
Shower door, surround:
Nathan Allan Glass
Studios Inc.
Vanity tops: Vitraform
integrated sinks,
countertops
Lights: Vibia
Plumbing supplies:
Grohe
Drawer pulls: Alexander
Marchant Specialty
Hardware
Shower: Hand-slumped
glass
Countertops: custom
glass integrated w/ sinks
Flooring: hand-hewn
marble

MARK CRAVOTTA, OF CRAVOTTA STUDIOS, IS RESPONSIBLE for bringing this Lake Austin home to life. Boasting modern style especially suited to the specific tastes of the client, the lakeside dwelling is an escape from the everyday. Inside this bath, an array of curves gives the space its unique ambiance. Such curvaceous elements include the cabinets and showers, which lend the room its contemporary aesthetic. All situated at different heights, the vanities and tub create stunning interest.

In addition to the unique coordination and connection issues, Cravotta incorporated glass countertops with integrated sinks atop cabinetry to create a light feel that bespeaks of quality. In the shower, hand-slumped glass adds another fantastic element. Each and every detail within the space is custom, resulting in beautiful craftsmanship and artistry throughout. A hand-hewn marble floor with rich depth enhances the textural qualities. Because the homeowners are avid readers, Cravotta incorporated hidden storage for books within the tub enclosure providing convenient access from inside the tub. The storage is integrated in the form of hidden drawers within the vanity, a convenience for the homeowners' daily bathtub reading time. «

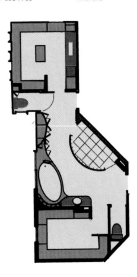

PHOTOGRAPHER: PAUL BARDAGJY

Newlywed Haven

DESIGNER
Dick Clark
Dick Clark Architecture
207 W. Fourth St.
Austin, TX 78701
512-472-4980

SPECIAL FEATURES
Large glass shower;
shower door goes to a
deck overlooking the
city; double Jacuzzi
stainless steel swooping
tub

DIMENSIONS
13' x 18'

PRODUCTS USED
Cabinetry: White oak
with natural finish, rift
cut, quarter sawn
Sinks: DCA Custom
stainless steel
Tub: Diamond Spas mid-
contour stainless steel
Toilet: Toto Carolina
Faucets: Dornbracht
Countertops, flooring:
Honed Antique Lueder
limestone
Hardware: Hafele
Backsplash: Rossi
USA Villebois Jaune
limestone
Walls: Chairo glass tiles
Millwork: Cerused oak
Ceiling: Marmarino
plaster
Stool: Custom by Emily
Summers, fabrication by
Gulassa & Co.
Rug: Van Bescow

WHO SAYS A HONEYMOON CAN'T LAST FOREVER?
When these newlyweds decided to remodel their
bathroom, they called on Dick Clark, of Texas-
based Dick Clark Architecture, to design a dream
space perfectly suited for romantic relaxing. One of
the couple's primary desires: to maintain the room's
exceptional view.

Thus the central focus of the bath is an enormous
all-glass shower, which opens directly to a large
outdoor deck, allowing the couple to move from the
shower to the sun-kissed outdoors in a matter of
seconds. The deck beautifully laces the house and
conveniently overlooks the city, providing the couple
with a great post-shower view.

Adjacent to the ceiling-mounted shower, Clark
incorporated separate sinks and vanity areas for each
spouse. Chiaro glass tiles surround
the room, which is connected to a vast
walk-in closet designed specifically for
the new couple. The completed space
now not only frames a stunning view
but provides the couple with ample
space to soak it all in. «

Lone Star Getaway

LOCATED IN DEL VALLE, TEXAS, this newly constructed home serves as a weekend getaway and boasts a modern ranch aesthetic throughout. Designed by David Webber, of Webber + Studio, Inc., the master bath is perhaps the epitome of the home's theme. When designing their bathroom, the homeowners' primary goal was to create a large, gracious room befitting a ranch house that would complement the décor of the home. Webber began construction on the large room by placing the tub at one end of the space. A walk-in shower imparts a sense of casual luxury, and a built-in lavatory near the tub adds a touch of style. To define privacy, Webber also created a water closet for the toilet.

A bay window, situated within one of the lengthened walls of the room, is just tall enough to fit a chair beneath. On either side of the window are his and her floating, open-room closets, providing the couple with a casual, comfortable place to prepare for the day or wind down for the night. Leather-paneled walls further contribute to the ranch feel of the home. The result is a warm, rich home, perfect for this large family—complete with children and grandchildren—to escape to when in need of a getaway. «

DESIGNER
David Webber
Webber + Studio, Inc.
300 West Ave., Suite 1322
Austin, TX 78701
512-236-1032

SPECIAL FEATURES
Bump-out closet;
window; leather walls;
rich pecan flooring;
copper sinks

DIMENSIONS
12' x 18'

PRODUCTS USED
Cabinetry: Arch Wood
Custom Cabinets
Flooring: Custom pecan
Countertops: Marble,
Architectural Tile and
Stone
Sinks: Rocky Mountain
Hardware
Tub: Kohler
Faucets: Waterworks
Lighting: Two Hills
Studio custom fixtures
Wallcovering: Custom
leather panels by Philip
Sell

PHOTOGRAPHER: PAUL BARDAGJY PHOTOGRAPHY

Marvelously Modern

WHEN THIS TEXAS HOMEOWNER decided it was time to update her bath area, she called on the design and architectural expertise of the team at McKinney Architects, Inc. Originally, the project was to consist of a gentle remodel intended to update the various finishes. In the end, however, the renovation went above and beyond.

Architects Al York, Heather McKinney, and Will Wood completely gutted the space. And though the fixtures remain in their previous location, such various main features as the cabinetry and the shower now occupy a prominent position.

A key to this special space is ample natural lighting. Light is emitted into the room above the tub, which provides a natural, relaxing atmosphere for the homeowner. The soaking tub is nestled perfectly into this comfort zone. The tub is also situated in the most visible location in the room, causing it to be the focal point and the premier recipient of natural light. The completed project left the homeowner happy with an exquisite place to unwind. «

DESIGNER
Al York, Heather
McKinney, Will Wood
McKinney Architects, Inc.
297 W. Eighth St.
Austin, TX 78701
512-476-0201

SPECIAL FEATURES
Shared natural lighting;
soaking tub

DIMENSIONS
16'6" x 10'6"

PRODUCTS USED
Casework: Walnut
Flooring: Honed slate
Sinks: Kohler
Tub: Japanese soaking
tub
Vanity tops: Honed slate
Faucets: Dornbracht
Other: Custom walnut
wrap at tub base

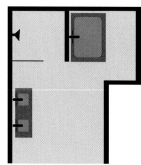

PHOTOGRAPHER: GREG HURSLEY

Bright Open Spaces

A MEMBER OF THE FASHION DESIGN WORLD, this homeowner recently relocated to an active-adult community in West Chester, Pennsylvania, and sought a designer who could improve her master bath without doing a total replacement. The homeowner already had a fabulous sauna, whirlpool tub, and beautiful tile floor, all of which were in excellent shape.

Working closely with the client, Conrad Muhly III, of Muhly K.B.A., evaluated the existing space and decided to increase the homeowner's storage capacity and improve the lighting in order to create a bright, airy space. A closet and small shower were removed and replaced with a large shower featuring porcelain-tile accent pieces and a tile ceiling. The shower base is adorned with striking mosaic tiles, bringing the look full-circle. The vanity from Kabinart is done in maple with a soft vanilla glaze finish, and the Corian countertops, Robern medicine cabinets, and Robern fluorescent lighting were incorporated to create a perfect reflection of sunlight.

Two 300-watt dimmable uplights and a crystal chandelier were also installed, and the current toilet and bidet were exchanged for new ones. In the end, the client was ecstatic with the open, bright, and comfortable look created by the designer at a reasonable price. «

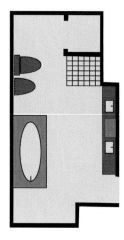

DESIGNER
Conrad E. Muhly III,
CKD, CBD
Muhly K.B.A., Inc.
7 North Five Points Road
West Chester, PA 19380
610-696-9191

SPECIAL FEATURES
Porcelain tile shower with mosaic floor; maple glazed cabinets; arched mirrors with vertical color-corrected lights

DIMENSIONS
23' x 12'

PRODUCTS USED
Tile: Florida Tile
Cabinetry: Kabinart
Mirrors: Robern Medicine Cabinets
Sink(s): DuPont Corian, Glacier White
Toilet: American Standard
Shower Door: Gordon Glass LTD, Custom Frameless
Vanity Tops: DuPont Corian, Cameo White
Lighting: Robern
Plumbing Supplies: Delta
Drawer Pulls: Cliffside Industries
Accessories: Smedbo Villa finish, chrome

PHOTOGRAPHER: DAVE GIFFORD OF GIFFORD IMAGES

Rocket Man's Retreat

WHEN A HOMEOWNER IS A ROCKET SCIENTIST by profession, one wouldn't expect anything less than a high-tech home. Such was the case for this L.A. homeowner, whose dwelling features a wide array of smart innovations. Among the many features, each room can be viewed from the homeowners' personal computers, and when away, they can call home to set the mood with music and lighting.

Despite so many creature comforts, the master bath needed a renovation. The problem was how to allow natural light in without compromising privacy. To cure the dilemma, designer Mark Schomisch cut a window behind the wall of the bathtub. To prevent prying eyes, he planted lush tropical foliage outside to block the view. He also selected brown mosaic tile for the tub and shower. A statuary white-marble slab tops a custom double vanity made of wood stained with ebony. Atop the counter, Schomisch installed white Kathryn sinks by Kohler, which complement the overall design of the bathroom.

Just outside, a tranquil Koi pond continues the interior aesthetic and is an inviting retreat for the busy homeowner. The pond is home to 12 fat, happy Koi and two tropical night-blooming water lilies. Because the homeowner works a traditional 9-to-5 job, the night-blooming flowers, which open after sunset and last into the morning, allow him to delight in the beauty of the garden. «

DESIGNER
Mark Schomisch

DIMENSIONS
15' x 13'

PRODUCTS USED
Tile: Bisazza brown mosaic
Cabinetry: Custom by Mark Schomisch
Sink(s): Kohler undermount
Faucet(s): American Brass
Toilet: Toto Supreme
Shower/tub fixtures: Axor
Countertops: Marble
Floors: Walker Zanger
Hardware: Details on La Cienega

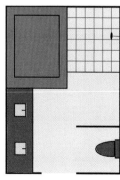

Fish Fantasy

Stewart Davis, of CG&S Design-Build, designed this exciting bath area when the Austin-based clients decided to build a tropical fantasy bathroom for their young daughter. This bath suite with a full bathroom and adjacent dressing area is specifically designed for the young daughter, dressed up in playful pastel colors and decorated with fanciful and fun fish tiles, creating a quaint little getaway for the little girl.

The original plan for this space was to give it a cosmetic upgrade with two side-by-side bath areas. However, during the preliminary stages of the redesign, the plans changed. The room now serves as a single, girl-oriented bath suite. The daughter's wing now features a hallway with bookshelves and storage leading into a dressing room, that has walk-in closet on either side. A pocket door with an opaque panel leads into the bath, which is painted with cool colors and features a river stone floor. An intricate glass-tile mosaic decorates the shower and sink area. «

DESIGNER
Stewart Davis
CG&S Design-Build
402 Corral Lane
Austin, TX 78745
512-444-1580

SPECIAL FEATURES
Dressing area; river stone floor; fish tiles

DIMENSIONS
6' x 9'

PRODUCTS USED
Cabinetry: Custom by Amazonia
Flooring: Island stone large pebble
Countertops: Gibraltar solid surfacing by Wilsonart
Sinks: Kohler Compass
Tub: Sunrise Speciality Co.
Tiles: Oceanside Glasstile, Pratt & Larson, Boyce & Bean glass mosaics

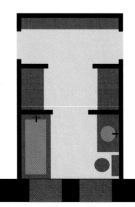

PHOTOGRAPHER: PETER TATA

Pebbled Pleasure

W HEN IT CAME TIME TO DESIGN THIS A USTIN , T EXAS , home and new bath space, Winn Wittman, of Winn Wittman Architecture, was ready to face the task. Achieving the clients' goal, this luxurious bath area flows into the bedroom while concurrently maintaining a formal air. There are no doors that separate the spaces, allowing for a smooth transition between the two areas. The only doors lead to an outdoor rock garden, creating a blur between outside and inside.

Mexican beach pebble is used inside to surround the granite tub, as well as outside to surround the stone path. This interesting correlation creates a dialogue between the spaces. The home is built with entertaining in mind, and the bath area in particular is designed with exceptional style and comfort. The bath is carved out of a single piece of granite, as are the polished sinks. The room has a view of the rock garden, as well as a rock wall carved out of the hill on which the house is built, where it sits in complete privacy. «

DESIGNER
Winn Wittman
Winn Wittman
Architecture
3601 South Congress
Ave., Bldg. B-500
Austin, TX 78704

SPECIAL FEATURES
Solid granite bathtub;
solid granite sinks

DIMENSIONS
19' x 10' 6"

PRODUCTS USED
Flooring: Black tile by
Master Tile of Austin
Countertops:
CaesarStone
Sinks: Solid granite by
Stone Forest
Faucets: Ferguson
Supply
Toilet: Wall-mounted,
double flush toilet
Tub: Solid granite by
Stone Forest
Shower Tiling: Hakatai
Enterprises
Shower Fixtures:
Ferguson Supply
Japanese Sliding Doors:
Wilkinson Woodworks,
Inc.

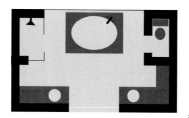

Vibrant Luxury

WHEN THE OWNERS OF THIS AUSTIN HOME decided it was time to remodel their existing bathroom, they called on the expertise of CG&S Design-Build's Stewart Davis. The team turned the shortage of space into an asset by relocating the adjacent closet and adding it to thep new room, breaking out the original 8-foot ceiling and creating a vaulted ceiling to the underside of the existing rafter.

To add a little more square footage to the space, the team also combined the tub and shower areas into an integrated bathing enclosure. The shower and tub area now boasts a two-person space with frameless glass doors. The toilet is positioned far into the room, while the sink is a point of interest upon entering the room.

For maximum volume and drama, the ceiling is raised to 16 feet. High windows, skylights, and cable lighting add much needed illumination. The framing of the ceilings and windows adds subtle sophistication to this elegant space. Vibrant colors and tiles add energy and dimension throughout the room. The contemporary style of the tech lighting, accent lighting, and solid-surface countertops contrast with artisan-style handmade tiles and warm cherry cabinets. Radiant floor heating, motorized windows and blinds, and a remote bath exhaust system add to the luxuriousness of the new bath. «

DESIGNER
Stewart Davis
CG&S Design-Build
402 Corral Lane
Austin, TX 78745
512-444-1580

SPECIAL FEATURES
Integrated bathing module; incorporation of attic space

DIMENSIONS
7' x 14'

PRODUCTS USED
Cabinetry: Custom by Amazonia
Flooring: Radiant by Warmly Yours
Countertops: Wilsonart
Faucets: Hansgrohe Terrano
Toilet: Toto
Lighting: Hera, Tech Lighting
Tub: Sunrise Specialty Co.
Tiles: Talisman, Oceanside, Pietri Bersage, Capco
Windows: Kolbe & Kolbe, Velux

Spa-Like Space

The owners of this quaint Austin, Texas, abode had the bath area of their new home envisioned, and it was up to John Hathaway, of Vanguard Studio, Inc., to transform their desires into a tangible living space. The bath boasts a large and luxurious presence, glistening with ample natural light and a beautiful view of the lake. Because the home site is very narrow, and has neighbors close to each side, the bath area is positioned in the center of the home as a special design element. The room's large windows visually enlarge the space and the lake view adds to the ambiance.

The shower itself is quite large. To allow the steamer to accommodate the entire shower, the ceilings had to be lowered. Now the relaxing element of steam adds to the spa-like atmosphere. The entire layout of the bathroom is configured in such a way that the whole family can get ready without space being an issue. An exercise room is also attached at one end of the area. The large windows are covered with a light fabric which allows for passage of some natural sunlight while being private enough to block neighboring views. «

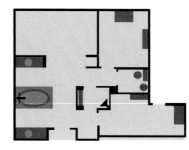

DESIGNER
John Hathaway
Vanguard Studio Inc.
6601 Vaught Ranch Rd.,
Ste. G-10
Austin, TX 78730
512-918-8312

SPECIAL FEATURES
Large windows with lake view from tub and vanities; attached exercise room with lake views

DIMENSIONS
15' x 16'

PRODUCTS USED
Cabinetry: Knotty Alder
Flooring: Granite
Countertops: Granite
Sinks: Undermounted porcelain
Faucets: Decorative wrought iron
Toilet: Comfort height with bidet
Lighting: Wrought iron old-world aged glass sconces
Tub: Deco mosaic deck whirlpool jetted spa tub
Wallcovering: Hand-painted faux finish with deco stencil
Shower: Mosaic granite with a rain dome and steamer

PHOTOGRAPHER: COLES HAIRSTON

Place of Perfection

WHEN IT CAME TIME TO DESIGN THIS GORGEOUS NEW HOME, it was up to John Hathaway, of Vanguard Studio, Inc., to turn the clients' dream into a reality. Hathaway was able to transform a small space into this glorious bath area. The high ceiling makes the room feel larger and more open, while luxurious state cabinetry keeps the space feeling like home. The room features a large walk-in shower, to the clients' delight. His and her vanities provide ample space for the homeowners. The area also features a makeup area, coffee bar, and television.

Onyx and mosaic tile patterns behind the floating master tub leave onlookers wowed by the beauty. The warm colors of the mosaic and the neutral tones of the walls and floor combine to add to the overall beauty of this space. The bath has a perimeter of beautiful columns and archways, which creates a classic theme to mirror the elegant fixtures and hardware. The tub itself is sure to leave onlookers breathless, as the body-hugging basin is a great place to unwind. To allow for maximum natural lighting, high punch windows are installed from both sides of the bathroom. The finished project achieves nothing less than perfection. «

DESIGNER
John Hathaway
Vanguard Studio, Inc.
6601 Vaught Ranch Rd.,
Ste. G-10
Austin, TX 78730
512-918-8312

SPECIAL FEATURES
High punch windows;
high ceilings

DIMENSIONS
15' x 18'

PRODUCTS USED
Cabinetry: Knotty Adler
(stained) by Burrows
Cabinetry
Flooring: Travertine by
Alkusari
Countertops: Granite
Sinks: Bar Clay
undermount
Faucets: Hans Grohe
oil-rubbed bronze
Toilet: Toto Drake
elongated
Lighting: Savoy oil-
rubbed bronze
Tub: Aquatic
Wallcovering: Sherwin
Williams hand-textured
Shower: Frameless glass
door travertine mosaic
Other: Onyx inlaid niche
behind tub

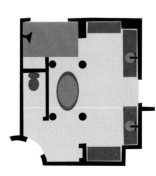

A Sight Unseen

OFTEN, A REMODELING PROJECT requires the designer to spend hours with the client, first in consultation, then in numerous trips to the site to ensure details are attended to and everyone is happy. However, there are exceptions. Marjorie Josselet, owner of Market House Kitchen & Bath Design Firm in Lee's Summit, Missouri, recently took on a project in which she did not see the room space until the project was complete.

The owner of this gorgeous home wanted a master suite that reflected her style. She wanted a much more traditional, Old World look than what she currently had. Most of the details were worked out during the initial consultation. She desired a clean design using granite and stone that was simple to clean. An Air Jet tub, new shower, and upgraded hardware on the cabinets were also included in the revamping of the bathroom.

The homeowner ordered a full suite of Delta plumbing products for the bathroom and decided to change the floor tile that was installed the previous year. The floor was updated to a travertine tile—the same material to be used on the shower walls, with granite accents to carry the countertop color onto the floor. «

DESIGNER
Marjorie Josselet
Market House Kitchen
& Bath
312 S.W. Market Street
Lee's Summit, MO 64063
816-246-8030

SPECIAL FEATURES
Accent tiles; Tralis Crema
Marfil & Corlis Crema
Marfil

DIMENSIONS
10' x 14'

PRODUCTS USED
Tile: Classico Travertine
Cabinetry: Custom
Sink(s): St. Thomas
Creations—Antigua
Petite
Tub: Ultra Bath Air Jet
Toilet: Toto
**Shower door &
Showerhead:** Delta
Victorian Collection
Sink faucets: Delta
Victorian Collection
Shower faucets: Delta
Vanity tops: Granite—
Antico Giallo
Plumbing: Delta bath
accessories—Victorian
Collection
Drawer pulls: Anne at
Home
Accessories: Hampton
Court Designs

Restful Retreat

THE RESIDENT OF AN OLDER HOME IN INDIANAPOLIS, this homeowner desired a large master bathroom to replace the smaller hallway bath. To transform what was an adjoining bedroom into a relaxing oasis, the homeowner brought in designer Michael Teipen.

Working with a blank canvas, Teipen's main challenge was determining where to place the main components—the shower, sinks, tub, and toilet. Following a brainstorming session with contractor Jimmy Dulin, the design team opted to place the shower and large, old-fashioned tub near the outer wall. Because trees and foliage blocked much of the natural light, they installed glass blocks to bring in additional light while providing privacy.

After removing the existing window, the opening was enlarged to provide an enchanting wall of illumination. To create interest and avoid a static feel, Teipen added angles to the shower entrances, on the corners of the sink cabinets, and on the newly created toilet enclosure. He selected tumbled marble to decorate the shower, backsplash, and flooring. Tying together the granite countertops, dark cabinet hardware, and cabinet glazing, the design team accentuated the main room with a "rug" composed of dark accent tiles. This beautiful bathroom now provides a restful retreat that the homeowner is sure to enjoy. «

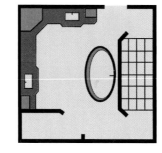

DESIGNER
Michael Teipen CMKBD,
Allied Member ASID
Kitchens By Teipen
1035 N. State Road 135
Greenwood, IN 46142
317-888-7345

SPECIAL FEATURES
Angled cabinets;
sink areas with upper
cabinets complete with
drawers; highlighted tile
pattern

DIMENSIONS
14'7" x 14'10"

PRODUCTS USED
Backsplash: Tumbled
marble
Flooring: Tumbled
marble
Cabinetry: Medallion,
cashew stain with
burnished glaze on
maple
Mirrors: Beveled glass
mirrors
Sinks: Kohler
Tub: Kohler
Toilet: Kohler
Vanity tops: Black
Galaxy granite
Faucets: Kohler
Drawer pulls: Top Knobs

Relaxing Curves

AFTER A LONG DAY OF MANAGING THE HECTIC SCHEDULES that comprise their days, this couple wanted a relaxing master bathroom where they could retreat from life's many demands. Inspired by a picture from a brochure, the homeowners tasked designer Marjorie Josselet, of Market House Kitchen & Bath Design, Lee's Summit, Missouri, with creating an inviting, relaxing space.

Josselet constructed the room with graceful steps leading to a large Jetta whirlpool set on an angle. A see-through fireplace and large, curved canopy add a measure of elegance to the space. Two columns flanking each side of the glass-block window top the marble as selected by the homeowner. Large double vanities include custom-made natural maple cabinets by Christiana Cabinetry with special custom countertops created by Grandview Tops, of Grandview, Missouri.

Additionally, Josselet crafted soft curves around the integrated sinks. These are topped off with a double bull-nose edge on Corian countertops, and they perch on each side of a curved knee space. Hidden in the lowered knee space is a lift-up makeup area, which is a perfect place for storing the all-important items necessary for getting ready in the morning. The space also provides an ideal spot to sit down and relax while putting on makeup. Curved chrome pulls from Top Knobs cap off the space with a charming finishing touch. «

DESIGNER:
Marjorie Josselet
Market House Kitchen &
Bath Design
312 S.W. Market St.
Lee's Summit, MO 64063
816-246-8030

SPECIAL FEATURES
Lift-up makeup area
with built-in mirror

DIMENSIONS:
12'6" x 19'3"

PRODUCTS USED
Tile: Field tile; marble
Cabinetry: Christiana
Cabinetry
Mirrors: Custom
Sink: Corian
Tub: Jetta Tub
Vanity Tops: Corian;
Abalone
Lights: Kovac; Pierce
Plumbing Supplies:
Delta Brizo
Drawer Pulls: Top Knobs

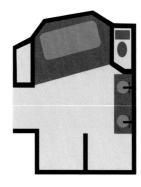

PHOTOGRAPHER: RUSSELL WALKER PHOTOGRAPHY

Request for Retreat

WHEN THESE TENNESSEE HOMEOWNERS decided to remodel their master bath, they informed Haskell "Hank" Matheny, of Haskell Interiors Design Collection, that the goal was a quiet retreat filled with luxury. They also said they didn't want to see the job until it was move-in ready. A French toile fabric from the client inspired the look and material selection for the renovation. Matheny gutted the bath down to the studs and made two changes to open the once-cramped space. First, he switched the original shower and tub, making the tub the centerpiece and leaving the shower tucked into a corner. Secondly, he moved the toilet into a portion of the original closet to create a private water closet.

To give the space a clean, up-to-date feeling, Matheny selected white marble, blue and green glass tile, and blue metallic paint for the surfaces. All this provides a calm, elegant background to the fixtures and furnishings. Such highly reflective materials as polished nickel, crystal, mirrors, and mirrored furniture add spark without fussiness. Matheny balanced the cool, light materials with touches of browns in the custom wood vanity, custom upholstery, and burl wood picture frames. Monograms, a faux lynx fur rug, and a crystal chandelier add glamour to room. Finally the owner's favorite antique sepia drawings take center stage. «

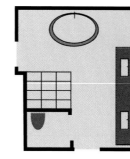

DESIGNER
Haskell "Hank" Matheny
Haskell Interiors Design Collection
85 First St. N.E.
Cleveland, TN 37311
423-472-6409

SPECIAL FEATURES
Custom carved vanity and backsplash; glass tile panels

DIMENSIONS
13' x 15'

PRODUCTS USED
Tile: Colorado Gold Vein Marble; Westminster trim; Akdo Beach Beach glass
Cabinetry: Kerns Wilcheck custom vanity
Mirrors: Custom w/ bevel
Sink(s): Toto
Tub: Bain Ultra Cella Air Tub
Toilet: Toto Promenade
Shower door: Custom enclosure with polished nickel handle
Vanity tops: Colorado Gold Vein parble
Lights: Haskell Interiors Design Collection private label
Plumbing supplies: Sigma faucets 2200 series
Drawer pulls: Cliffside, satin nickel
Drapery: Thiabut
Wallcovering: Benjamin Moore metallic paint

PHOTOGRAPHER: STEPHEN GREENFIELD

Residential Retreat

When designer Barry Miller first met with these Danbury, Connecticut, homeowners, they wanted to transform their 1950s master bathroom into a contemporary, luxurious space. Knowing they would be living in the home for years, the couple combined a modern aesthetic with a spa-like feel. To achieve the desired result, Miller eliminated a small linen closet in the hallway. Adding a mere 3 extra square feet of space allowed for a comfortable atmosphere and inspiring features. The new master bath boasts a roomy 6-by-3-foot shower stall with a dual showerhead and four body jets. A glass block window allows natural light into the space, and white-pebble glass tiles accent the shower floor. Just an arm's length away, warm towels and a heated tile floor entice the homeowners.

A one-piece clear glass countertop and sink is beautifully accented by lighted candles beneath, and the iridescent black tile on one full wall with coordinating accent strips dramatically contrasts the white wall tile. The contemporary theme offers maximum comfort and functionality. Not only is the new master bath more efficient and luxurious, but visitors tell the homeowners it belongs at a resort. «

DESIGNER
Simply Baths
A Division of The Brush's
End
37A Padanaram Road
Danbury, CT 06811
866-NUBATH1

SPECIAL FEATURES
Spacious shower stall
with dual showerhead
and four body jets;
glass countertops, sink;
iridescent black tile wall

DIMENSIONS
6'8'' x 10'7''

PRODUCTS USED
Tile: Vitrium glass
Cabinetry: Ove Décor
Mirrors: Ove Décor
Sink(s): Ove Décor
Faucet(s): Danze
Toilet: Kohler
Shower door: Custom
frameless
Shower floor: Daltile
glass pebble
Radiant heat: Warmly
yours

Forever Elegant

THIS BATHROOM BELONGS TO A SINGLE, young New York man. The continuity of the classic design and elements designer Guita Behbin tried to achieve are very clear, especially because like many apartments, this one is in a classic New York City pre-war neighborhood. The bath was given a gut facelift, lifting the tile line all the way up to the ceiling with the most beautiful variety of shapes and sizes of classic Carrara Marble. As if in a formal living room, the walls are trimmed with traditionally carved and detailed marble baseboard, chair rail, and crown moulding to top it all off. Between the chair rail and the crown, Behbin had a very large-scale, masculine version of the "subway" tile pattern. Keeping to classic undying design in this bathroom was important, as it fulfilled the client's wish to create the feeling that it had always been there in his pre-war apartment. The juxtaposition of the beautiful light walls and floors with the dark, rich-stained traditional cherry was a winning formula. The richness of the woodwork was not left only to the vanity, but it was extended to the medicine cabinet, which matches the vanity. The bathroom doors were stripped and stained to match as well, especially because the moulding detail of the original doors are the same as the new cabinetry. To complete and complement this classic design, Behbin chose traditionally styled, polished chrome fixtures and accessories to accommodate the client's need for contemporary comfort. «

DESIGNER:
Guita Behbin
Dura Maid
Industries, Inc.
130 Madison Avenue
New York, NY 10016
212-686-0246

SPECIAL FEATURES:
All white marble bath with carved mouldings in marble and rich cherry wood work

DIMENSIONS:
5' x 9'

PRODUCTS USED:
Tile: White Carrara marble
Cabinetry: Wood-Mode
Sink(s): Kohler
Tub: Kohler
Toilet: Kohler
Shower Door: Coastal Industries
Showerhead: Aquadis
Sink Faucets: Aquadis
Shower Faucets: Aquadis
Vanity Tops: White Carrara marble
Lights: Task
Plumbing Supplies: Aquadis
Drawer Pulls: Top Knobs

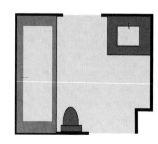

PHOTOGRAPHER: STEVE WHITSITT

Contempo-Cool

THE OWNERS OF THIS 17-YEAR-OLD HOME IN LISLE, ILLINOIS, faced a design dilemma that plagues many homeowners: a bathroom with a small, confining shower and large unused tub. The owners knew the bathroom had the potential to be an oasis in the middle of their home, and they recruited Jessica A. Gomes, of Casa Bella Design Center, to tackle the project.

Gomes created a unique layout that reworked the room's problem areas. The designer devised a multilevel, freestanding tub highlighted by a six-inch platform. A tile panel neatly houses the gleaming nickel fixtures. Gomes also incorporated a larger shower that was completely repositioned to provide privacy without a door or curtain.

The designer employed clean lines and cool hues throughout the room, giving it a contemporary feel. She accented the architectural features by using varying tile sizes and configurations. She also endeavored to give the existing cabinets a facelift with a new Impala Black granite countertop. The new vessel basins and wall-mounted faucets match the 12-inch backsplash. The room's soothing blue walls are the final touch that transformed this once utilitarian room into a relaxing refuge where the homeowners can now happily unwind at the end of the day. «

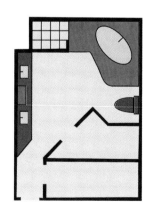

DESIGNER:
Jessica A. Gomes
Casa Bella Design Center
15 W. Jefferson, Suite 103
Naperville, IL 60540
630-718-1440

SPECIAL FEATURES:
Multilevel flooring; walk-in shower; freestanding tub; custom tub control wall; wall-mounted faucets; vessel sinks

DIMENSIONS:
16' x 23'

PRODUCTS USED:
Tile: Pavimenti Litogres; Ekos Stone Argilla
Cabinetry: Existing cabinets with maple custom insert
Mirrors: Custom
Sink: Kohler
Tub: Jason
Toilet: Kohler
Vanity tops: Granite
Lights: Six-inch can lighting
Plumbing supplies: Kohler

MEMBER OF
SEN DESIGN GROUP

PHOTOGRAPHER: SHERMAN DUNNAM

Steam For Two

When Colleen Thompson, of Blau Bath & Kitchens, met with her clients for the first time, they expressed their dream for a renewed bathroom space evoking clean, simple lines much like one would find in a neo-classic design. Specifically, they longed for a steam shower built for two with multiple showerheads, a large whirlpool, additional lighting, as well as display space for her artwork. All this without touching their existing sauna or expanding into their master bedroom suite.

Thompson met her clients' needs by using all-natural materials, while maintaining a contemporary simplicity of style throughout. The new bath space included a smooth black granite vanity top with an undermounted bowl and a shelf across the bidet and toilet, travertine marble on the shower walls, tub deck, heated floor and wainscoting, and a custom clear-glass steam enclosure to keep the space open. Cherry cabinetry with a wheat stain was selected, accented by faucetry and bath accessories sporting a satin nickel finish with copper metallic tile inserts and cabinet hardware.

The result of this divine reconfiguration is a welcoming, soothing and accessible escape for the homeowners to unwind… whether together, or alone. «

DESIGNER
Colleen Thompson
Blau Bath and Kitchen,
1320 South 108th St.
Milwaukee, WI 53214
414-259-1030

SPECIAL FEATURES
Steam shower with dual shower heads; whirlpool tub for two; travertine marble deco with insert tiles

DIMENSIONS
42' x 20'

PRODUCTS USED
Tile: Travertine Marble with Metal Deco Inserts
Cabinetry: Jay Rambo Wexford Cherry with Wheat Stain
Mirrors: Robern Recessed Cabinet Framed Mirrors
Sink: Kohler Undermount Caxton
Tub: Hydroswirl Orcas
Toilet: Kohler San Raphael - Biscuit
Shower Door: Custom Clear Glass with Chrome Trim
Sink Faucets: Artistic Brass Satin Nickel
Shower Faucets: Artistic Brass Satin Nickel
Vanity Tops: Granite - Galaxy Black
Lights: Hale Recessed Ceiling Lights with White Baffle;
Drawer Pulls: Ann Sacks Caracol
Other: Artistic Brass - Satin Nickel

Borrowed Space

FROM WHAT WAS ONCE A TYPICAL 5 X 8-FOOT POWDER ROOM, designer Fara Boico of Classic Kitchen & Bath Center, Ltd., successfully created a subdued retreat for the owners of this Long Island home.

By borrowing space from an adjacent closet and an unused bedroom, she was able to more than double the room's size, enabling the addition of a whirlpool tub, separate shower, and a host of other amenities. The expansive vanity, with its bumped out sink, features a custom angled Corian top as well as an undermount sink. Cabinets flanking the vanity provide ample storage for toiletries, linens, and other supplies. A knee wall separates the vanity and corner shower, helping to maintain the room's expansive feel.

Tucked neatly into a corner, the shower includes body sprays, a thermostat control to regulate and maintain water temperature, and separate water volume controls. The specially selected ceramic tile, which flows throughout the shower walls and floor, provides a look and feel of tumbled marble, while the handmade triangular border adds a customized design detail.

With an eye toward safety, Boico selected a whirlpool tub with integral grab bars, while protecting privacy with a smartly tucked toilet into its own corner nook. Such attention to detail successfully transformed a small and ordinary powder room into an expanded retreat where relaxation is the number one priority. «

DESIGNER
Fara Boico
Classic Kitchen and Bath Center
1062 Northern Boulevard
Roslyn, NY 11576
516-621-7700

SPECIAL FEATURES
Angled vanity cabinet arrangement; frameless shower doors; whirlpool built into deck; custom designed tile border; corian top with undermount sink

DIMENSIONS
9' x 10'

PRODUCTS USED
Tile: 6" x 6" matte texture with customer border
Cabinetry: Kountry Kfaft Pickeled Birch stain
Mirrors: Once piece, no seams over vanity area
Sink(s): Kohler, Caxton undermount
Tub: Whirlpool – Jacuzzi
Toilet: Kohler Rialto
Shower Door: Custom frameless with satin nickel finish
Showerhead: Rain
Sink faucets: Sepco
Vanity Tops: Corian
Lights: Recessed high hats
Drawer pulls: Satin nickel

PHOTOGRAPHER: BILL ROTHSCHILD

Max Convenience

DESCRIBED AS TOO SMALL AND CRAMPED by its homeowners, the existing postage-stamp sized master bath was barely adequate for one person. The challenge presented to Laura Jensen CKD, CKB, of The Kitchen Guide, was to enlarge the space to accommodate two people.

The designer met this challenge by utilizing the corridor between the bath and the closet adding seven feet to the bath and allowing enough space for a 3 x 4½-foot shower. Pushing out the wall behind the existing vanity by just 1 foot created sufficient width to accommodate his and her sinks in opposite corners.

With the bathroom now enlarged, the designer needed to make the still modest-size room appear even larger. She used the same faux marble tile on the floors and walls to create a sense of visual continuity. The wall-mounted sinks topped with granite maximize floor space. To keep additional weight off the sinks, the tops were cemented in place on 4-inch thick walls, further held in place by mirrors.

Finishing touches include matte and polished chrome trims, glass shelves bonded to the mirrors, recessed outlets in the bottoms of the cabinets, and a magazine rack. Additionally, the elimination of the old closet required a partial redesign of the master bedroom, which now includes two walk-in closets. «

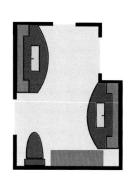

DESIGNER
Laura M. Jensen, CKD, CBD
The Kitchen Guide Inc
25834 North Knollwood Dr.
Barrington, IL 60100
847-487-7075

SPECIAL FEATURES
Wall-mount sinks with granite overlay; optically bonded glass shelves; same tile on wall and floor for uniform background; magazine rack inside of tall cabinet; recessed lights under cabinet bottoms; blend of matte and chrome trim

DIMENSIONS
7' x 12'

PRODUCTS USED
Tile: Himalaya Makuda;
Cabinetry: Plato, Norwood II door style, Parchment on cherry;
Mirrors: Custom with optically bonded glass shelves
Sinks: Kohler Cabernet wall mount, Tender Gray
Toilet: Kohler, San Raphael, Tender Grey
Shower door: Basco
Showerhead: Hans grohe, KWC Valve
Sink faucets: Newport
Vanity tops: Cold Springs Granite - Royal Mahogany
Lights: Ron Rezek Florescent strips / Halogen Puck Lites
Drawer pulls: Hafele, Matte and Pol Chrome Combo
Other: Sky Tube

PHOTOGRAPHER: MARA

Heightened Allure

DESIGNER
Rick Ruzanski
Detailed Builders, Inc.
417 Quentin Rd
Palatine, IL 60067
847-991-9586

SPECIAL FEATURES
Elegant multi-head
shower with steam
unit; heavy sealed glass
door; Jacuzzi Presage
whirlpool; multi-height
lavatory and sink basin
countertops.

DIMENSIONS
9' x 9'6"

Products Used
Tile: Magica Beige
with Castel cap;
Cabinetry: Amera–
Avondale
Mirrors: Broan recessed
medicine cabinet
Sink: Corian Lavatory
#820
Tub: Jacuzzi Presage.
Toilet: Kohler Portrait
Bisquit
Sink Faucets: Barclay
Accessories: Victoria
Collection in polished
brass
Shower Faucets: Grohe
components in polished
brass
Vanity Tops: Corian
Vanilla with Glacier
White lavatory sink
basins
Drawer Pulls: Cliffside
Industries

THE OWNERS OF THIS LATE 1980S TRACK HOME DECIDED
it was time to transform the existing master bathroom into a
luxurious sanctuary in which to relax and unwind.

Working within a limited amount of space, Randy
Ruzanski, professional designer with Distinctive Home
Improvements, Inc., rose to the challenge by introducing
luxury amenities, transforming this room into a customized escape.

Paying attention to the multi-height needs of the
homeowners, the bath area contains an elegant multi-
head shower with an Amerec steam unit enclosed within
a heavy glass door, as well as multi-height mirrors and
glass throughout the room. The Jacuzzi-Presage whirlpool
bathtub, multi-height lavatory, and sink basin countertops
further create unmatched comfort and convenience.

Attention to every amenity is exemplified in the Grohe
polished-brass shower faucetry, solid-
surface vanity countertops, and iron
drawer pulls and door knobs. Brass towel-
bar accessories, the bisquit-colored toilet,
and the shower faucets and showerhead
in brass add just the right accents to this
divine retreat, creating a room that is both
serene and stimulating. Enjoying this spa-
like retreat is the best way to begin or end
any day! «

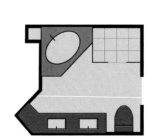

PHOTOGRAPHER: JEFFREY ROSEN

APPENDIX
BATH TEMPLATES

Lavatories

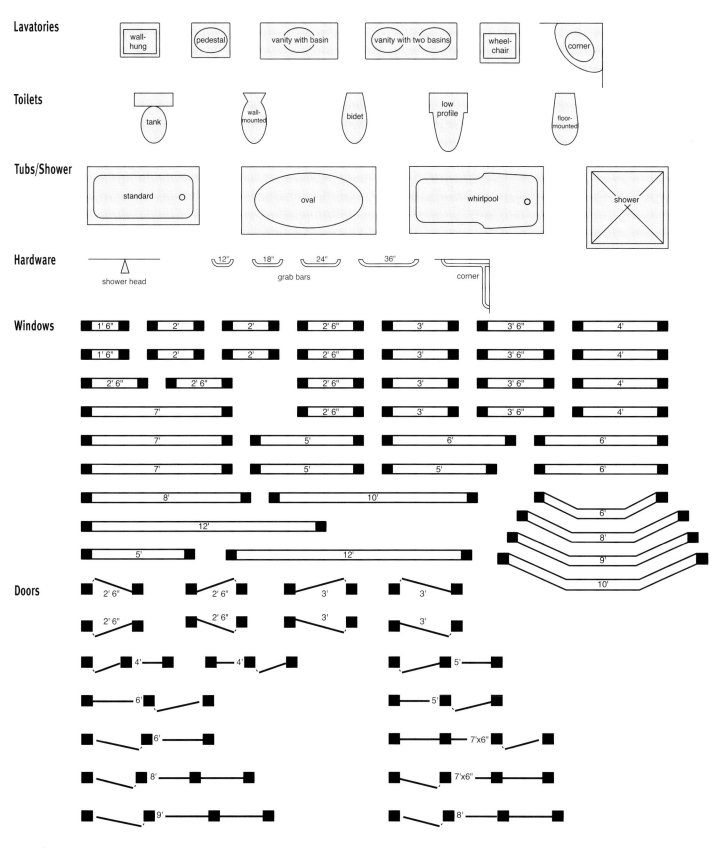

wall-hung · pedestal · vanity with basin · vanity with two basins · wheel-chair · corner

Toilets

tank · wall-mounted · bidet · low profile · floor-mounted

Tubs/Shower

standard · oval · whirlpool · shower

Hardware

shower head · grab bars 12" 18" 24" 36" · corner

Windows

1' 6" · 2' · 2' · 2' 6" · 3' · 3' 6" · 4'
1' 6" · 2' · 2' · 2' 6" · 3' · 3' 6" · 4'
2' 6" · 2' 6" · 2' 6" · 3' · 3' 6" · 4'
7' · 2' 6" · 3' · 3' 6" · 4'
7' · 5' · 6' · 6'
7' · 5' · 5' · 6'
8' · 10' · 6'
12' · 8'
5' · 12' · 9'
10'

Doors

2' 6" · 2' 6" · 3' · 3'
2' 6" · 2' 6" · 3' · 3'
4' · 4' · 5'
6' · 5'
6' · 7'x6"
8' · 7'x6"
9' · 8'

Scale: 1 square=1 foot

BASIC BATHROOM PLANNING GUIDELINES

According to the National Kitchen & Bath Association (NKBA), there are over 40 million pre-existing houses in the United States. Very often, these homes contain a typical-sized 5- x 7-foot bathroom. That doesn't leave much space for more than a standard tub, toilet, and lavatory, so professional designers encourage remodelers to expand these small baths to accommodate more amenities and to provide greater space for maneuvering safely and comfortably. The NKBA has developed a comprehensive list of bathroom planning guidelines that help both bath design professionals and homeowners who are designing a bath remodel on their own—whether or not expansion is an option. These guidelines appear here with the expressed permission of the NKBA.

1a. Doorways at least 32 inches wide and not more than 24 inches deep in the direction of travel.

1b. The clear space at a doorway must be measured at the narrowest point.

1c. Walkways should be a minimum of 36 inches wide.

2. Clear floor space at least the width of the door on the push side and a larger clear floor space on the pull side for maneuvering to open, close, and pass through the doorway.

3. A minimum clear floor space of 30 x 48 inches either parallel or perpendicular should be provided at the lavatory.

4a. A minimum clear floor space of 48 x 48 inches provided in front of the toilet with 16 inches of that clear floor space extending to each side of the fixture's centerline.

4b. Up to 12 inches of the 48 x 48 inches of clear floor space can extend under the lavatory when total access to a knee space is provided.

5. A minimum clear floor space of 48 x 48 inches from the front of the bidet should be provided.

6a. A minimum clear floor space of 60 x 30 inches at the bathtub for a parallel approach.

6b. A minimum clear floor space of 60 x 48 inches at the bathtub for a perpendicular approach.

7. A minimum clear floor space at a shower less than 60 inches wide should be 36 inches deep x shower width + 12 inches. A shower 60 inches wide or greater requires a space of 36 inches deep x shower width.

8. The clear floor spaces required at each fixture may overlap.

9. Turning space of 180 degrees planned for in the bathroom. Minimum diameter of 60 inches for 360-degree turns and/or T-turn with a space of 36 x 36 x 60 inches.

10. A minimum clear floor space of 30 x 48 inches is required beyond the door swing in the bathroom.

11. For more than one vanity, one may be 30–34 inches and another 34–42 inches high.

12. Kneespace provided at the lavatory, 27 inches above the floor at the front edge and 30 inches wide.

13. The bottom edge of the mirror over the lavatory should be a maximum of 40 inches above the floor or a maximum of 48 inches above the floor if it is tilted.

14. The minimum clear floor space from the centerline of the lavatory to any side wall is 15 inches.

15. The minimum clearance between two bowls in the lavatory center is 30 inches, centerline to centerline.

16. In an enclosed shower, the minimum usable interior dimensions are 34 x 34 inches measured wall to wall.

17. Showers should include a bench or seat that is 17–19 inches above the floor and a minimum of 15 inches deep.

18. A 60-inch shower requires a 32-inch entrance. If the shower is 42 inches deep, 36 inches is required.

19. Shower doors must open into the bathroom.

20. No steps at the tub or shower area. Safety rails should be installed to facilitate transfer.

21. All showerheads equipped with a pressure-balance/temperance regulator or temperature-limiting device.

22a. Shower controls accessible from inside and outside the fixture and located between 38–48 inches above the floor and offset toward the room.

22b. Tub controls accessible from inside and outside the fixture and located between the tub rim and 33 inches above the floor, below the grab bar and offset toward room.

23a. A minimum 16-inch clearance from the centerline of the toilet or bidet to any obstruction on either side.

23b. For adjacent toilet and bidet installation, the 16-inch minimum clearance to all obstructions should be maintained.

24. The toilet-paper holder installed within reach of person seated on the toilet, slightly in front of the edge of the toilet and centered 26 inches above the floor.

25. Compartmentalized toilet areas should be a minimum of 36 x 66 inches with a swing-out door or pocket door.

26. Walls reinforced to receive grab bars in the tub, shower, and toilet areas.

27. Storage for toiletries, linens, grooming, and general bathroom supplies provided 15–48 inches above the floor.

28. Storage for soap, towels, and personal hygiene items should be installed within reach of person seated on bidet or toilet or within 15–48 inches above the floor and do not interfere with use of fixture.

29. In the tub/shower area, storage for soap and personal hygiene items provided with 15–48 inches above the floor.

30. All flooring should be slip-resistant.

31. Exposed pipes and mechanicals covered by protective panel or shroud.

32. Controls, dispensers, outlets, and operating mechanisms 15–48 inches above the floor and operable with a closed fist.

33. Access panel to all mechanical, electrical, and plumbing systems.

34. Mechanical ventilation systems included to vent entire room. Calculation for minimum size of system: Cubic space (L x W x H) x 8 (changes per hour) = minimum cubic feet per minute (CFM) 60 minutes

35. Ground fault circuit interrupters specified on all receptacles, lights, and switches. All light fixtures above the tub/shower must be moisture-proof, special-purpose fixtures.

36. Auxiliary heating may be planned in an addition to the primary heat source.

37. Every function should be well illuminated with task lighting, night lights, and/or general lighting. No lighting fixtures should be within reach of person seated or standing in tub or shower.

38. Bathroom lighting should include a window/skylight area equal to a minimum of 10 percent of bathroom's square footage.

39. Controls, handles, and door/drawer pulls should be operable with one hand, require minimal strength, and do not require tight grasp, pinching, or twisting of wrist.

40. Use clipped or radius corners for open countertops and eased to eliminate sharp edges.

41. Any glass in a tub/shower partition or other glass application within 18 inches of the floor should be laminated glass with a plastic interlayer, tempered glass, or approved plastic.

Have a home decorating, improvement, or gardening project? Look for these and other fine Creative Homeowner books wherever books are sold.

All you need to know about maximizing the space you have. Over 275 photos. 256 pp.; 9¼"×10⅞"
BOOK #: 279031

How to work with space, color, pattern, and texture. Over 400 photos. 288 pp.; 9¼"×10⅞"
BOOK #: 279679

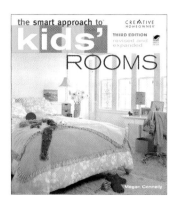

Ideas for furnishing and decorating space for children. Over 300 color photos. 224 pp.; 9¼"×10⅞"
BOOK #: 279961

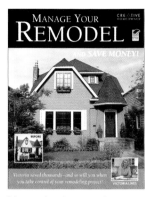

How to be the general contractor on a large-scale remodel. Over 220 color photos. 192 pp.; 8½"×10⅞"
BOOK #: 277874

A visual reference guide to color ideas for kitchens and baths. Over 300 color photos. 304 pp., 7"×9¼"
BOOK #: 279648

Update and add style to your home using paint. Over 275 photos. 208 pp.; 8½"×10⅞"
BOOK #: 279575

Inspiration for creating an attractive, up-to-date kitchen. Over 500 color photos. 224 pp.; 8½"×10⅞"
BOOK #: 279412

Information on the latest trends in design and materials. Over 500 color photos. 224 pp.; 8½"×10⅞"
BOOK #: 279261

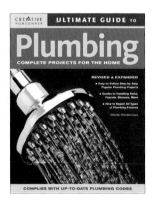

The complete manual for all plumbing projects. Over 800 color photos. 288 pp.; 8½"×10⅞"
BOOK #: 278200

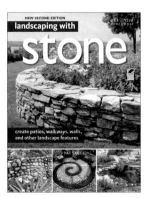

Ideas for incorporating stone into the landscape. Over 400 photos & illustrations. 224 pp.; 8½"×10⅞"
BOOK #: 274179

Grow your own fruit and vegetables. Over 300 color photos & illustrations. 224 pp.; 8½"×10⅞"
BOOK #: 274557

Information to improve gardening knowledge. More than 450 photos. 256 pp.; 8½"×10⅞"
BOOK #: 274183

For more information and to place an order, go to **www.creativehomeowner.com**